3

FOUR CORNERS

Second Edition

Student's Book
with Online Self-Study

JACK C. RICHARDS & DAVID BOHLKE

CAMBRIDGE
UNIVERSITY PRESS

CAMBRIDGE
UNIVERSITY PRESS & ASSESSMENT

Shaftesbury Road, Cambridge CB2 8EA, United Kingdom

One Liberty Plaza, 20th Floor, New York, NY 10006, USA

477 Williamstown Road, Port Melbourne, VIC 3207, Australia

314–321, 3rd Floor, Plot 3, Splendor Forum, Jasola District Centre, New Delhi – 110025, India

103 Penang Road, #05–06/07, Visioncrest Commercial, Singapore 238467

Cambridge University Press & Assessment is a department of the University of Cambridge.

We share the University's mission to contribute to society through the pursuit of education, learning and research at the highest international levels of excellence.

www.cambridge.org
Information on this title: www.cambridge.org/fourcorners

First published 2012
Second edition 2019

20 19 18 17

Printed in Brazil by Forma Certa Grafica Digital LTDA

A catalogue record for this publication is available from the British Library

ISBN 978-1-108-55859-4 Student's Book with Online Self-Study 3
ISBN 978-1-108-55980-5 Student's Book with Online Self-Study 3A
ISBN 978-1-108-55982-9 Student's Book with Online Self-Study 3B
ISBN 978-1-108-61762-8 Student's Book with Online Self-Study and Online Workbook 3
ISBN 978-1-108-65810-2 Student's Book with Online Self-Study and Online Workbook 3A
ISBN 978-1-108-67667-0 Student's Book with Online Self-Study and Online Workbook 3B
ISBN 978-1-108-45935-8 Workbook 3
ISBN 978-1-108-46076-7 Workbook 3A
ISBN 978-1-108-45936-5 Workbook 3B
ISBN 978-1-108-55995-9 Teacher's Edition with Complete Assessment Program 3
ISBN 978-1-108-55999-7 Full Contact with Online Self-Study 3
ISBN 978-1-108-56013-9 Full Contact with Online Self-Study 3A
ISBN 978-1-108-562-928 Full Contact with Online Self-Study 3B
ISBN 978-1-108-45940-2 Presentation Plus Level 3

Additional resources for this publication at www.cambridge.org/fourcorners

Authors' acknowledgments

Many people contributed to the development of *Four Corners*. The authors and publisher would like to particularly thank the following **reviewers**:

Nele Noe, **Academy for Educational Development, Qatar Independent Secondary School for Girls**, Doha, Qatar; Pablo Stucchi, **Antonio Raimondi School** and **Instituto San Ignacio de Loyola**, Lima, Peru; Nadeen Katz, **Asia University**, Tokyo, Japan; Tim Vandenhoek, **Asia University**, Tokyo, Japan; Celso Frade and Sonia Maria Baccari de Godoy, **Associação Alumni**, São Paulo, Brazil; Rosane Bandeira, **Atlanta Idiomas**, Manaus, Brazil; Cacilda Reis da Silva, **Atlanta Idiomas**, Manaus, Brazil; Gretta Sicsu, **Atlanta Idiomas**, Manaus, Brazil; Naila Maria Cañiso Ferreira, **Atlanta Idiomas**, Manaus, Brazil; Hothnã Moraes de Souza Neto, **Atlanta Idiomas**, Manaus, Brazil; Jacqueline Kurtzious, **Atlanta Idiomas**, Manaus, Brazil; José Menezes Ribeiro Neto, **Atlanta Idiomas**, Manaus, Brazil; Sheila Ribeiro Cordeiro, **Atlanta Idiomas**, Manaus, Brazil; Juliana Fernandes, **Atlanta Idiomas**, Manaus, Brazil; Aline Alexandrina da Silva, **Atlanta Idiomas**, Manaus, Brazil; Kari Miller, **Binational Center**, Quito, Ecuador; Alex K. Oliveira, **Boston University**, Boston, MA, USA; Noriko Furuya, **Bunka Gakuen University**, Tokyo, Japan; Robert Hickling, **Bunka Gakuen University**, Tokyo, Japan; John D. Owen, **Bunka Gakuen University**, Tokyo, Japan; Elisabeth Blom, **Casa Thomas Jefferson**, Brasília, Brazil; Lucilena Oliveira Andrade, **Centro Cultural Brasil Estados Unidos (CCBEU Belém)**, Belém, Brazil; Marcelo Franco Borges, **Centro Cultural Brasil Estados Unidos (CCBEU Belém)**, Belém, Brazil; Geysa de Azevedo Moreira, **Centro Cultural Brasil Estados Unidos (CCBEU Belém)**, Belém, Brazil; Anderson Felipe Barbosa Negrão, **Centro Cultural Brasil Estados Unidos (CCBEU Belém)**, Belém, Brazil; Henry Grant, **CCBEU – Campinas**, Campinas, Brazil; Maria do Rosário, **CCBEU – Franca**, Franca, Brazil; Ane Cibele Palma, **CCBEU Inter Americano**, Curitiba, Brazil; Elen Flavia Penques da Costa, **Centro de Cultura Idiomas – Taubaté**, Taubaté, Brazil; Inara Lúcia Castillo Couto, **CEL LEP – São Paulo**, São Paulo, Brazil; Sonia Patricia Cardoso, **Centro de Idiomas Universidad Manuela Beltrán**, Barrio Cedritos, Colombia; Geraldine Itiago Losada, **Centro Universitario Grupo Sol (Musali)**, Mexico City, Mexico; Nick Hilmers, **DePaul University**, Chicago, IL, USA; Monica L. Montemayor Menchaca, **EDIMSA**, Metepec, Mexico; Angela Whitby, **Edu-Idiomas Language School**, Cholula, Puebla, Mexico; Mary Segovia, **El Monte Rosemead Adult School**, Rosemead, CA, USA; Dr. Deborah Aldred, **ELS Language Centers, Middle East Region**, Abu Dhabi, United Arab Emirates; Leslie Lott, **Embassy CES**, Ft. Lauderdale, FL, USA; M. Martha Lengeling, **Escuela de Idiomas**, Guanajuato, Mexico; Pablo Frias, **Escuela de Idiomas UNAPEC**, Santo Domingo, Dominican Republic; Tracy Vanderhoek, **ESL Language Center**, Toronto, Canada; Kris Vicca and Michael McCollister, **Feng Chia University**, Taichung, Taiwan; Flávia Patricia do Nascimento Martins, **First Idiomas**, Sorocaba, Brazil; Andrea Taylor, **Florida State University in Panama**, Panamá, Panama; Carlos Lizárraga González, **Groupo Educativo Angloamericano**, Mexico City, Mexico; Bo-Kyung Lee, **Hankuk University of Foreign Studies**, Seoul, South Korea; Dr. Martin Endley, **Hanyang University**, Seoul, South Korea; Mauro Luiz Pinheiro, **IBEU Ceará**, Ceará, Brazil; Ana Lúcia da Costa Maia de Almeida, **IBEU Copacabana**, Copacabana, Brazil; Maristela Silva, **ICBEU Manaus**, Manaus, Brazil; Magaly Mendes Lemos, **ICBEU São José dos Campos**, São José dos Campos, Brazil; Augusto Pelligrini Filho, **ICBEU São Luis**, São Luis, Brazil; Leonardo Mercado, **ICPNA**, Lima, Peru; Lucia Rangel Lugo, **Instituto Tecnológico de San Luis Potosí**, San Luis Potosí, Mexico; Maria Guadalupe Hernández Lozada, **Instituto Tecnológico de Tlalnepantla**, Tlalnepantla de Baz, Mexico; Karen Stewart, **International House Veracruz**, Veracruz, Mexico; Tom David, **Japan College of Foreign Languages**, Tokyo, Japan; Andy Burki, **Korea University, International Foreign Language School**, Seoul, South Korea; Jinseo Noh, **Kwangwoon University**, Seoul, South Korea; Neil Donachey, **La Salle Junior and Senior High School**, Kagoshima, Japan; Rich Hollingworth, **La Salle Junior and Senior High School**, Kagoshima, Japan; Quentin Kum, **La Salle Junior and Senior High School**, Kagoshima, Japan; Geoff Oliver, **La Salle Junior and Senior High School**, Kagoshima, Japan; Martin Williams, **La Salle Junior and Senior High School**, Kagoshima, Japan; Nadezhda Nazarenko, **Lone Star College**, Houston, TX, USA; Carolyn Ho, **Lone Star College-Cy-Fair**, Cypress, TX, USA; Kaoru Kuwajima, **Meijo University**, Nogoya, Japan; Alice Ya-fen Chou, **National Taiwan University of Science and Technology**, Taipei, Taiwan; Raymond Dreyer, **Northern Essex Community College**, Lawrence, MA, USA; Mary Keter Terzian Megale, **One Way Línguas-Suzano**, São Paulo, Brazil; B. Greg Dunne, **Osaka Shoin Women's University**, Higashi-Osaka, Japan; Robert Maran, **Osaka Shoin Women's University**, Higashi-Osaka, Japan; Bonnie Cheeseman, **Pasadena Community College** and **UCLA American Language Center**, Los Angeles, CA, USA; Simon Banha, **Phil Young's English School**, Curitiba, Brazil; Oh Jun Il, **Pukyong National University**, Busan, South Korea; Carmen Gehrke, **Quatrum English Schools**, Porto Alegre, Brazil; John Duplice, **Rikkyo University**, Tokyo, Japan; Mengjiao Wu, **Shanghai Maritime University**, Shanghai, China; Wilzania da Silva Nascimento, **Senac**, Manaus, Brazil; Miva Silva Kingston, **Senac**, Manaus, Brazil; Lais Lima, **Senac**, Manaus, Brazil; Yuan-hsun Chuang, **Soo Chow University**, Taipei, Taiwan; Wen hsiang Su, **Shih Chien University Kaohsiung Campus**, Kaohsiung, Taiwan; Lynne Kim, **Sun Moon University (Institute for Language Education)**, Cheon An City, Chung Nam, South Korea; Regina Ramalho, **Talken English School**, Curitiba, Brazil; Tatiana Mendonça, **Talken English School**, Curitiba, Brazil; Ricardo Todeschini, **Talken English School**, Curitiba, Brazil; Monica Carvalho da Rocha, **Talken English School**, Joinville, Brazil; Karina Schoene, **Talken English School**, Joinville, Brazil; Diaña Peña Munoz and Zira Kuri, **The Anglo**, Mexico City, Mexico; Christopher Modell, **Tokai University**, Tokyo, Japan; Song-won Kim, **TTI (Teacher's Training Institute)**, Seoul, South Korea; Nancy Alarcón, **UNAM FES Zaragoza Language Center**, Mexico City, Mexico; Laura Emilia Fierro López, **Universidad Autónoma de Baja California**, Mexicali, Mexico; María del Rocío Domínguez Gaona, **Universidad Autónoma de Baja California**, Tijuana, Mexico; Saul Santos Garcia, **Universidad Autónoma de Nayarit**, Nayarit, Mexico;Christian Meléndez, **Universidad Católica de El Salvador**, San Salvador, El Salvador; Irasema Mora Pablo, **Universidad de Guanajuato**, Guanajuato, Mexico; Alberto Peto, **Universidad de Oaxaca**, Tehuantepec, Mexico; Carolina Rodriguez Beltan, **Universidad Manuela Beltrán, Centro Colombo Americano**, and **Universidad Jorge Tadeo Lozano**, Bogotá, Colombia; Nidia Milena Molina Rodriguez, **Universidad Manuela Beltrán** and **Universidad Militar Nueva Granada**, Bogotá, Colombia; Yolima Perez Arias, **Universidad Nacional de Colombia**, Bogotá, Colombia; Héctor Vázquez García, **Universidad Nacional Autónoma de Mexico**, Mexico City, Mexico; Pilar Barrera, **Universidad Técnica de Ambato**, Ambato, Ecuador; Doborah Hulston, **University of Regina**, Regina, Canada; Rebecca J. Shelton, **Valparaiso University, Interlink Language Center**, Valparaiso, IN, USA; Tae Lee, **Yonsei University**, Seodaemun-gu, Seoul, South Korea; Claudia Thereza Nascimento Mendes, **York Language Institute**, Rio de Janeiro, Brazil; Jamila Jenny Hakam, **ELT Consultant**, Muscat, Oman; Stephanie Smith, **ELT Consultant**, Austin, TX, USA.

Scope and sequence

LEVEL 3	Learning outcomes	Grammar	Vocabulary
Classroom language Page 2			
Unit 1 Pages 3–12			
Education **A** *I'm taking six classes* **B** *You're not allowed to…* **C** *My behavior* **D** *Education controversy*	**Students can…** ✓ ask and talk about routines ✓ express prohibition and obligation ✓ ask and talk about feelings and reactions ✓ discuss advantages and disadvantages	Simple present vs. present continuous Zero conditional	School subjects Feelings and emotions
Unit 2 Pages 13–22			
Personal stories **A** *What were you doing?* **B** *Guess what!* **C** *I was really frightened!* **D** *How embarrassing!*	**Students can…** ✓ describe what was happening in the past ✓ announce news ✓ close a conversation ✓ tell personal stories ✓ describe embarrassing moments	Past continuous vs. simple past Participial adjectives	Sentence adverbs Verbs to describe reactions
Unit 3 Pages 23–32			
Style and fashion **A** *Fashion trends* **B** *Does this come in…?* **C** *The latest look* **D** *Views on fashion*	**Students can…** ✓ ask about and describe past fashions ✓ ask where something is in a store ✓ ask for a specific product ✓ express opinions about style and fashion ✓ ask and talk about current fashions	*Used to* Defining relative clauses	Fashion statements Clothing styles
Unit 4 Pages 33–42			
Interesting lives **A** *Have you ever been on TV?* **B** *What I mean is…* **C** *Life experiences* **D** *What a life!*	**Students can…** ✓ ask and talk about life experiences ✓ check and clarify meaning ✓ describe details of their experiences ✓ ask and talk about a memorable experience	Present perfect Present perfect vs. simple past	Experiences Fun things to do
Unit 5 Pages 43–52			
Our world **A** *Older, taller, and more famous* **B** *I don't believe it!* **C** *World geography* **D** *Natural wonders*	**Students can…** ✓ Compare human-made structures ✓ express disbelief ✓ say that they don't know something ✓ ask and talk about geographical features ✓ describe natural wonders in their country	Comparatives *Not as…as* Superlatives	Human-made wonders Geographical features
Unit 6 Pages 53–62			
Organizing your time **A** *A busy week* **B** *Can I take a message?* **C** *Can you do me a favor?* **D** *Perspectives on time*	**Students can…** ✓ ask and talk about weekend plans ✓ offer to take a message ✓ leave a message ✓ make requests, promises, and offers ✓ discuss ways to manage time effectively	Present tenses used for future Requests Promises and offers with *will*	Commitments Favors

Functional language	Listening and Pronunciation	Reading and Writing	Speaking
Interactions: Expressing prohibition Expressing obligation	**Listening:** Office rules An interview about homeschooling **Pronunciation:** Stress and rhythm	**Reading:** "Are Video Games Educational?" An article **Writing:** Advantages and disadvantages of distance education	• Information exchange about school and work • *Keep talking*: "Find someone who" activity about everyday activities • List of class rules • Information exchange about personal behavior • *Keep talking*: Comparison of behaviors • Discussion about distance education
Interactions: Announcing news Closing a conversation	**Listening:** News about other people A camping trip **Pronunciation:** Intonation in complex sentences	**Reading:** "Embarrassing Experiences" An article **Writing:** An embarrassing moment	• Group story about a past event • *Keep talking*: Description of simultaneous past actions • Celebrity news • Personal stories and anecdotes • *Keep talking*: Picture stories • Descriptions of embarrassing moments
Interactions: Asking where things are Asking for an alternative	**Listening:** Clothing purchases An interview with a fashion designer **Pronunciation:** *Used to* and *use to*	**Reading:** "Dress to Impress" An article **Writing:** Class survey	• Interview about style and fashion • *Keep talking*: Comparison of two people's past and present styles • Role play of a shopping situation • Opinions on fashion and style • *Keep talking*: Interview about what's hot • Class survey about style and fashion
Interactions: Checking meaning Clarifying meaning	**Listening:** Unusual habits An interview with a grandmother **Pronunciation:** Contrastive stress in responses	**Reading:** "The Life of an Astronaut" An interview **Writing:** Interesting people, places, or things	• Interview about experiences • *Keep talking*: Information exchange about experiences never had • Information exchange about unusual habits • True and false information about life experiences • *Keep talking*: "Find someone who" activity about everyday experiences • Description of an interesting person or place
Interactions: Expressing disbelief Saying you don't know	**Listening:** An interesting city The Great Barrier Reef **Pronunciation:** Intonation in tag questions	**Reading:** "Seven Wonders of the Natural World" An article **Writing:** A natural wonder	• Comparison of different places • *Keep talking*: Information gap activity about impressive places • Information exchange about human-made structures • Discussion about experiences in different places • *Keep talking*: Advice for foreign visitors • List of the most wonderful places in the country
Interactions: Offering to take a message Leaving a message	**Listening:** Weekend plans Phone messages **Pronunciation:** Reduction of *could you* and *would you*	**Reading:** "Time and Culture" An article **Writing:** Tips for success	• "Find someone who" activity about weekend plans • *Keep talking:* Information exchange about upcoming plans • Role play with phone messages • Class favors, offers, and promises • *Keep talking*: Role play with requests • Quiz about overdoing things

LEVEL 3	Learning outcomes	Grammar	Vocabulary
Unit 7 Pages 63–72			
Personalities **A** *You're extremely curious.* **B** *In my opinion, . . .* **C** *We've been friends for six years.* **D** *What is your personality?*	**Students can...** ✓ talk about personality traits ✓ give an opinion ✓ ask for agreement ✓ describe people's personalities ✓ talk about their personalities	Adverbs modifying adjectives and verbs Present perfect with *for* and *since*	Personality traits More personality traits
Unit 8 Pages 73–82			
The environment **A** *Going green* **B** *I'd rather not say.* **C** *What will happen?* **D** *Finding solutions*	**Students can...** ✓ discuss environmental problems ✓ give an approximate answer ✓ avoid answering ✓ talk about future possibilities ✓ discuss solutions to problems	Quantifiers First conditional	Environmental impacts Tips to help the environment
Unit 9 Pages 83–92			
Relationships **A** *Healthy relationships* **B** *I'm really sorry.* **C** *That can't be the problem.* **D** *Getting advice*	**Students can...** ✓ discuss what's important in relationships ✓ apologize and give excuses ✓ accept an apology ✓ speculate about people ✓ give advice about relationships	*It's . . .* expressions Expressions with infinitives Modals for speculating	Relationship behaviors Inseparable phrasal verbs
Unit 10 Pages 93–102			
Living your life **A** *He taught himself.* **B** *I'll give it some thought.* **C** *What would you do?* **D** *What an accomplishment!*	**Students can...** ✓ talk about themselves and their experiences ✓ advise against something ✓ consider advice ✓ talk about imaginary situations ✓ ask and talk about accomplishments	Reflexive pronouns Second conditional	Qualities for success Separable phrasal verbs
Unit 11 Pages 103–112			
Music **A** *Music trivia* **B** *The first thing you do is . . .* **C** *Music and me* **D** *Making your own music*	**Students can...** ✓ talk about music ✓ give instructions ✓ talk about things they've done recently ✓ talk about memorable songs	Past passive Present perfect with *yet* and *already*	Compound adjectives Verb and noun formation
Unit 12 Pages 113–122			
On vacation **A** *Travel preferences* **B** *Don't forget to...* **C** *Rules and recommendations* **D** *Seeing the sights*	**Students can...** ✓ discuss travel preferences ✓ ask about preferences ✓ remind someone of something ✓ talk about rules and recommendations ✓ describe their dream trip	Gerunds Modals for necessity and recommendations	Vacation activities Extreme sports

Functional language	Listening and Pronunciation	Reading and Writing	Speaking
Interactions: Giving an opinion Asking for agreement	**Listening:** Common proverbs A personality quiz **Pronunciation:** Reduction of *don't you*	**Reading:** "The Signs of the Zodiac" Descriptions **Writing:** My personality	• Interview about personality traits • *Keep talking*: "Left-brain vs. right-brain" quiz • Discussion about personality assumptions • Information exchange about friends and their personalities • *Keep talking*: Interviews about special people and things • Guessing game to match people and their personality descriptions
Interactions: Giving an approximate answer Avoiding answering	**Listening:** A survey on grocery shopping habits Award winners for environmental work **Pronunciation:** Stress in compound nouns	**Reading:** "One-of-a-Kind Homes" An article **Writing:** A letter about an environmental issue	• Discussion about community environmental problems • *Keep talking*: "Green" quiz • Survey about water usage • Cause and effect • *Keep talking*: Possible outcomes in different situations • Solutions to environmental issues
Interactions: Apologizing Accepting an apology	**Listening:** Apologetic phone calls A radio call-in show **Pronunciation:** Sentence stress	**Reading:** "Addy's Advice" Emails **Writing:** A piece of advice	• Tips for healthy relationships • *Keep talking*: Advice for relationship problems • Role play to apologize and make excuses • Speculations about classmates • *Keep talking*: Speculations about people • Discussion about relationship problems
Interactions: Advising against something Considering advice	**Listening:** Three problems Interviews about accomplishments **Pronunciation:** Stress shifts	**Reading:** "A Walk Across Japan" An interview **Writing:** An accomplishment	• Interview about personal experiences • *Keep talking*: "Find someone who" activity about personal experiences • Role play to give and consider advice • Discussion about hypothetical situations • *Keep talking*: Interview about hypothetical situations • "Find someone who" activity about accomplishments
Interactions: Beginning instructions Continuing instructions Ending instructions	**Listening:** How things work Song dedications **Pronunciation:** Syllable stress	**Reading:** "A Guide to Breaking into the Music Business" A guide **Writing:** A music review	• Guessing game about music • *Keep talking*: Discussion about music • Information exchange with instructions • "Find someone who" activity about recent actions • *Keep talking*: "Find the differences" activity about two friends • Information exchange about songs and memories
Interactions: Asking about preferences Reminding someone of something	**Listening:** Hotel check-in A white-water rafting trip **Pronunciation:** Reduction of verbs	**Reading:** "A Taste of Cairo" A food blog **Writing:** A walking tour	• Interview about vacation activities • *Keep talking*: Comparison of travel preferences • Role play about checking into a hotel • Discussion about extreme sports • *Keep talking*: Plan for a backpacking trip • Information exchange about dream trips

Classroom language

A Complete the conversations with the correct sentences. Then listen and check your answers.

What page are we on?	✓ Excuse me. I'm very sorry I'm late.
Can you repeat that, please?	May I go to the restroom, please?
What's our homework?	Which role do you want to play?

A *Excuse me. I'm sorry I'm late.*

B That's OK. Next time try to arrive on time.

A ______________________

B Thirteen. We're doing the Warm-up for Unit 2.

A ______________________

B Yes. I said, "Please work with a partner."

A ______________________

B I'll be Student A. You can be Student B.

A ______________________

B No problem. Please try to be quick.

A ______________________

B Please complete the activities for Unit 2 in your workbook.

B PAIR WORK Practice the conversations.

1 Education

Lesson A
- School subjects
- Simple present vs. present continuous

Lesson B
- Expressing prohibition
- Expressing obligation

Lesson C
- Feelings and emotions
- Zero conditional

Lesson D
- Reading "Are Video Games Educational?"
- Writing: Distance education

Warm Up

A Describe the pictures. What do you see? What are the students doing?

B How are the classrooms similar or different from your own classroom experiences?

A I'm taking six classes.

1 Vocabulary School subjects

A 🎧 **Match the words and the pictures. Then listen and check your answers.**

a algebra
b art
c biology
d chemistry
e geometry
f history
g music
✓h physics
i world geography

1 h 

2 ☐ 

3 ☐ 

4 ☐ 

5 ☐ 

6 ☐ 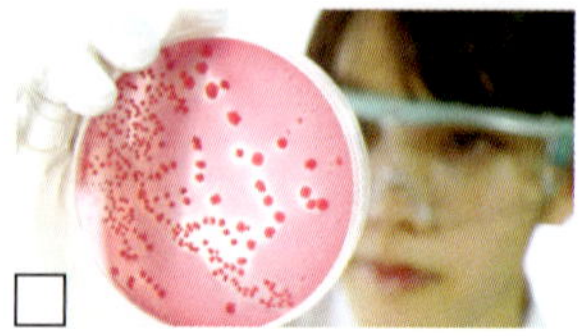

7 ☐ 

8 ☐ 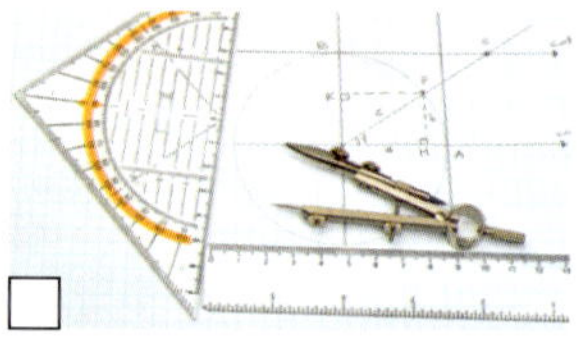

9 ☐ 

B 🎧 **Complete the chart with the correct school subjects. Then listen and check your answers.**

Arts	Math	Science	Social studies
art			

C PAIR WORK **Which school subjects are or were easy for you? Which are or were difficult? Tell your partner.**

"History and music were easy subjects for me, but algebra was difficult!"

2 Language in context Busy schedules

A 🎧 **Listen to three people talk about their schedules. Who doesn't have a job?**

I'm a high school student. I love history and world geography. I have a part-time job, too. My parents own a restaurant, so I work there on Saturdays. I guess I'm pretty busy. *–Kenji*

I'm a full-time student. I want to be a doctor. I'm taking six classes and preparing for my medical school entrance exams. I study biology and chemistry every night. *–Jan*

I'm really busy! I work full-time at a bank. I'm also taking an English class at night with my friend Ricardo. Actually, I'm going to class now. I think I'm late! *–Amelia*

B **What about you? Do you have a busy schedule? What do you do in a typical week?**

3 Grammar Simple present vs. present continuous

Use the simple present to describe routines and permanent situations.
Kenji **works** on Saturdays.
Jan **studies** every night.
Kenji's parents **own** a restaurant.

Use the present continuous to describe actions in progress or temporary situations.
Amelia **is going** to class right now.
Jan **is preparing** for her medical school entrance exams.
Amelia and Ricardo **are taking** an English class together.

Verbs not usually used in continuous tenses

believe	mean
have	own
hope	remember
know	seem
like	understand
love	want

A **Complete the conversations with the simple present or present continuous forms of the verbs. Then practice with a partner.**

1 A ___Are___ you ___taking___ (take) a lot of classes these days?
B I ________ (take) just two: world geography and physics. I ________ (have) a full-time job, so I ________ (not / have) a lot of free time.

2 A How often ________ you ________ (go) to the library?
B I ________ (go) every Saturday. But I ________ (study) at home a lot, too. I ________ (prepare) for an important exam.

3 A How ________ (be) your English class?
B It ________ (be) fine. I ________ (like) English and ________ (want) to improve my speaking. But we ________ (be) only in the first lesson!

4 A What ________ the teacher ________ (do) now?
B She ________ (help) some students. They ________ (ask) her questions. They ________ (seem) confused about something.

B PAIR WORK **Ask and answer the questions in Part A. Answer with your own information.**

4 Speaking School and work

A PAIR WORK **Read the list. Add one set of questions about school or work.**

- What's your favorite class? Are you learning anything interesting?
- Do you have a job? If so, what do you do?
- Are you studying for any exams? Do you study alone or with others?
- What job do you want someday? Are you doing anything to prepare for it?
- Why are you studying English? What do you hope to do in this class?
- ________? ________?

B GROUP WORK **Share any interesting information from Part A.**

5 Keep talking!

Go to page 123 for more practice.

I can ask and talk about routines.

B You're not allowed to . . .

1 Interactions Prohibition and obligation

A Do you always follow rules? Do you ever break rules? If so, when?

B Listen to the conversation. What *can* students do in the class? Then practice the conversation.

Justin Excuse me. Do you mind if I sit here?
Fei Not at all. Go ahead.
Justin Thanks. I'm Justin, by the way.
Fei Hi. I'm Fei. Are you new in this class?
Justin Yeah. Today is my first day. Hey, can we drink coffee in class?
Fei No. You can't eat or drink in class. It's one of the rules.
Justin Really? Good to know.
Fei Oh, and there's another rule. You have to turn off your cell phone.
Justin OK. Thanks for letting me know.
Fei Sure. Do you want to be my language partner today? We can choose our speaking partners in this class.
Justin OK. Thanks.

C Read the expressions below. Complete each box with a similar expression from the conversation. Then listen and check your answers.

Expressing prohibition	Expressing obligation
You can't . . .	______
You're not allowed to . . .	You need to . . .
You're not permitted to . . .	You must . . .

D PAIR WORK Look at the common signs. Say the rules. Take turns.

"You're not permitted to park here."

2 Listening First day at work

A Listen to Joel's co-workers explain the office rules on his first day at work. Number the pictures from 1 to 6.

B Listen again. Write the office rules.

1 ______________________ 4 ______________________

2 ______________________ 5 ______________________

3 ______________________ 6 ______________________

3 Speaking Class rules

A PAIR WORK Make a list of five important rules for your class like the one below.

Class rules

1. You must raise your hand to speak.
2. You can't send or read text messages.
3. You have to turn off your cell phone.
4. You're not permitted to chew gum.
5. You're allowed to sit anywhere you want.

B GROUP WORK Compare your list with another pair. Choose the five most important rules.

C CLASS ACTIVITY Share your lists. Can you and your teacher agree on a list of class rules?

I can express prohibition and obligation.

C My behavior

1 Vocabulary Feelings and emotions

A Match the words and the pictures. Then listen and check your answers.

a	angry	c	hungry	e	lonely	g	scared	i	thirsty
b	busy	d	jealous	f	nervous	h	sleepy	j	upset

B PAIR WORK Why do you think the people in the pictures feel the way they do? Discuss your ideas.

2 Conversation Feeling nervous

A Listen to the conversation. Why is Nate eating so late?

Nate Hello?

Laura Hi, Nate. It's Laura. Are you busy?

Nate Not really. I'm just eating some ice cream.

Laura Really? Why are you eating so late?

Nate Oh, I have an exam tomorrow, and I'm kind of nervous about it. I eat when I'm nervous. I'm not even hungry! It's not good, I know.

Laura Well, a lot of people eat when they're nervous. If I'm nervous about something, I just try not to think about it.

Nate That's easier said than done! But what do you do if you have a really important exam?

Laura I study a lot, of course!

B Listen to the rest of the conversation. Why did Laura call Nate?

3 Grammar Zero conditional

Zero conditional sentences describe things that are generally true. Use the simple present for both the if *clause (the condition) and the main clause.*

What **do** you **do** if you **have** a really important exam?

If I **have** a really important exam, I **study** a lot.

I **study** a lot if I **have** a really important exam.

You can usually substitute when *for* if *in zero conditional sentences.*

If I'm nervous about something, I just try not to think about it.

When I'm nervous about something, I just try not to think about it.

A **Match the conditions and the main clauses. Then compare with a partner.**

1 If I'm nervous before an exam, ______
2 When I'm busy with chores at home, ______
3 If I wake up and feel hungry, ______
4 When I get angry at someone, ______
5 If my friends don't call me for a few days, ______
6 When I feel sleepy on Sunday mornings, ______

a. I ask a family member to do some.
b. I start to get lonely.
c. I have something healthy, like an apple.
d. I usually don't say anything to him or her.
e. I like to stay in bed.
f. I take a deep breath and try to relax.

B PAIR WORK **Make true sentences about your behavior with the conditions in Part A. Tell your partner.**

"If I'm nervous before an exam, I study with a friend."

4 Pronunciation Stress and rhythm

A **Listen and repeat. Notice how stressed words occur with a regular rhythm.**

When I'm **lonely**, I **like** to **chat** or **talk** on the **phone** with my **friends**.

B PAIR WORK **Practice the sentences from Exercise 3A. Pay attention to your stress and rhythm.**

5 Speaking Different behaviors

GROUP WORK **Read the list. Add two more questions with *if* or *when*. Then ask and answer them.**

- What do you do if you feel sleepy in class?
- What do you do when you get jealous?
- How do you feel when you're alone at night?
- How do you feel when you speak English in class?
- ________________
- ________________

6 Keep talking!

Go to page 124 for more practice.

I can ask and talk about feelings and reactions.

D Education controversy

1 Reading

A Do you think video games can be educational? Why or why not?

B Read the article. What do many parents feel about video games?

Are video games educational?

Many parents have a bad feeling about video games. Some believe that if they allow their children to play video games, they won't do well in school. Others feel that too many video games, especially violent ones, make children feel angry and nervous. If their kids spend a lot of time playing games alone, some parents are afraid that they will feel lonely and have a hard time making friends.

But recent studies suggest a more positive side to video games, and that video games are helping students to learn, to make friends and to build important skills.

One of the biggest advantages of playing video games is that they give the brain a great workout. Every gamer knows that when you are playing video games, you have to think fast and make decisions quickly. In some really hard games, players have to learn how to form strategies, plan their actions and manage their time. Studies also show that many video games are helping students to improve math and reading skills.

Video games can also bring students together and help them make friends. In multiplayer games, players must work with their team to achieve a goal. Some games give players a chance to be leaders and increase their confidence.

Physically, scientists believe that video games may help to manage stress, improve eyesight and increase hand-eye coordination.

In many ways, video games are helping to make learning new skills more fun. Perhaps someday, video games will be a bigger part of a student's education.

C Read the article again. Complete the chart by listing three skills that video games can help students build in each area.

Cognitive (Thinking) Skills	Social skills	Physical skills
improve time management skills	learn to work with a team	

D PAIR WORK What kind of video games do you think are educational? Do you think video games can be played in classrooms? Tell your partner.

2 Listening Is homeschooling for you?

A Listen to Julie and her parents discuss homeschooling. What do they like about it, and what are their challenges? Check (✓) the correct answers.

	Likes	Challenges	Advice
Julie	☐ the classroom ☐ the hours ☐ the teachers	☐ texting friends ☐ not seeing friends in class ☐ being in a real school	
Julie's parents	☐ teaching together ☐ choosing the curriculum ☐ working at home	☐ scheduling ☐ giving grades ☐ knowing every subject	

B Listen again. What advice do Julie and her parents give to people considering homeschooling? Complete the chart with their advice.

3 Writing Distance education

A PAIR WORK Read the definition of distance education. Then make a list of its advantages and disadvantages.

Distance education is a type of education where students work on their own at home and communicate with teachers and other students using email, message boards, instant messaging, video chats, and other forms of computer-based communication.

B Do you think learning English by distance education is a good idea or a bad idea? Write a paragraph to explain your opinion. Use the model and your list from Part A.

Advantages of Distance Education

I think learning English by distance education is a very good idea. There are many advantages. For example, students can work at their own speed. This is good for people with full-time jobs or people who can't go to regular classes . . .

C PAIR WORK Compare your ideas.

4 Speaking Advantages and disadvantages

A GROUP WORK What are the advantages and disadvantages of these types of learning? Discuss your ideas.

large classes	private lessons with a tutor	studying abroad
small classes	online learning	watching movies in English

B CLASS ACTIVITY How do you prefer to learn? What type of learning is the most popular?

I can discuss advantages and disadvantages.

Wrap-up

1 Quick pair review

Lesson A Do you remember?

Cross out the word that doesn't belong. Then write the category. You have two minutes.

1	math	algebra	~~history~~	geometry
2		art	history	world geography
3		music	art	algebra
4		biology	geometry	chemistry

Lesson B Guess!

Think of a place that has rules. Tell your partner things you can and can't do there, but don't say the name of the place. Can your partner guess it? You have two minutes.

A: You're not permitted to talk. You must turn off your cell phone.

B: Is it a library?

Lesson C Find out!

What is one thing both you and your partner do in each situation? You have three minutes.

- What do you do if you feel scared?
- What do you do if you get a phone call in class?
- What do you do if you have a lot of homework?

A: If I'm scared, I turn on the lights. Do you?

B: No. I lock the doors if I'm scared. Do you?

A: Yes.

Lesson D Give your opinion!

What are two advantages and two disadvantages of taking a class online? You have three minutes.

2 In the real world

What is a multi-age classroom? Go online and find information in English about one. Then write about it.

- What ages or grades are in the classroom?
- What are some advantages? What are some disadvantages?

A Multi-Age Classroom

At Ambuehl Elementary School, first-, second-, and third-graders are in the same classroom. One advantage is that younger students learn from older students. Another advantage is that . . .

2 Personal stories

Lesson A
- Sentence adverbs
- Past continuous vs. simple past

Lesson B
- Announcing news
- Closing a conversation

Lesson C
- Verbs to describe reactions
- Participial adjectives

Lesson D
- Reading: "Embarrassing Experiences"
- Writing: An embarrassing moment

Warm Up

A Look at the pictures. Which story would you like to hear? Rank them from 1 (very much) to 6 (not much).

B Do you prefer to tell stories about yourself or hear stories about other people? Why?

A What were you doing?

1 Vocabulary Sentence adverbs

A Match the pictures and the sentences. Then listen and check your answers.

1 
2 
3 
4 

_____ **Amazingly**, she came home last night.

_____ **Fortunately**, she was very healthy.

_____ **Sadly**, my cat disappeared last year.

_____ **Strangely**, she had on a little sweater.

5 
6 
7 
8 

_____ **Luckily**, someone found it.

_____ **Suddenly**, I realized I didn't have it.

_____ **Surprisingly**, she brought it to my home.

_____ **Unfortunately**, I lost my wallet yesterday.

B PAIR WORK Use sentence adverbs to describe incidents that happened to you or people you know. Tell your partner.

"Amazingly, my brother passed his physics exam last week. He didn't study at all!"

2 Language in context Lights out!

A Listen to two people describe what they were doing when the power went out last night. What did they do after the power went out?

I was cooking pasta when suddenly everything went dark. Luckily, I had some candles. I couldn't finish making my meal, so I just ate cereal for dinner.

– Angela

While my friends and I were watching a movie at home, the lights went out. Unfortunately, no one knew how the movie ended. So, we took turns telling our own endings.

– Tetsu

B What about you? Have you ever been in a blackout? What did you do?

3 Grammar Past continuous vs. simple past

Use the past continuous to describe an action in progress in the past.

Angela **was cooking** pasta last night. Tetsu and his friends **were watching** a movie.

Use the simple past for an event that interrupts that action in progress.

Angela **was cooking** pasta when everything **went** dark.

While Tetsu and his friends **were watching** a movie, the lights **went** out.

A Complete the conversations with the past continuous or simple past forms of the verbs. Then practice with a partner.

1 A What *were* you *doing* (do) last night when the storm ________ (begin)?
B I ________ (use) my computer. While I ________ (write) my report, the electricity suddenly ________ (go) off.
A ________ you ________ (lose) your work?
B Yeah. Unfortunately, I ________ (need) to do it again.

2 A How ________ you ________ (break) your foot?
B Oh, I ________ (ski).
A Really? ________ it ________ (hurt)?
B Of course! But fortunately, someone ________ (call) an ambulance.
A That's good.
B Yeah, and while I ________ (wait), my friends ________ (bring) me hot chocolate.

B PAIR WORK **Ask and answer questions about what you were doing at the times below.**

7:00 this morning 10:00 last night 4:30 yesterday afternoon this time yesterday

4 Pronunciation Intonation in complex sentences

Listen and repeat. Notice how each clause has its own intonation pattern.

Angela was cooking pasta when everything went dark.

When everything went dark, Angela was cooking pasta.

5 Speaking Story time

GROUP WORK **Complete a sentence below with your own idea. Your group adds sentences with adverbs to create a story. Take turns.**

- I was talking to my best friend when . . .
- I was sleeping one night when . . .
- I was walking down the street when . . .
- I was checking my messages when . . .

A: *I was talking to my best friend when my phone rang.*

B: *Strangely, it was a phone number I didn't know.*

C: *Luckily, I answered the phone because it was . . .*

6 Keep talking!

Go to page 125 for more practice.

I can describe what was happening in the past.

B Guess what!

1 Interactions Sharing news

A Think about different people you know. Do you have any news about them?

B Listen to the conversation. What news is Diana sharing? Then practice the conversation.

Ruben	Hi, Diana. How are you?
Diana	I'm fine. Guess what!
Ruben	What?
Diana	Do you remember Joe from our photography class?
Ruben	Joe? Oh, yeah. Is he OK?
Diana	Oh, he's fine. It's just that he got into film school in Los Angeles. He wants to be a director.
Ruben	Really? Good for him.
Diana	Yeah. I hear he really likes it.
Ruben	That's fantastic!
Diana	Yeah. Hey, I need to get going. I'm late for work.
Ruben	Oh, OK. I'll call you later.

C Read the expressions below. Complete each box with a similar expression from the conversation. Then listen and check your answers.

Announcing news

____

Did you hear what happened?

You'll never guess what happened!

Closing a conversation

____

Listen, I've got to run.

Sorry, I have to go.

D PAIR WORK Have conversations like the one in Part B. Use these ideas.

Your classmate Lucy Kim moved away. She moved to Spain to study art.

Your teacher Bill Jones got married. He married his girlfriend from high school.

Your friend Pedro Garcia was on TV. He was on a game show and won!

2 Listening You'll never guess!

A **Listen to Michael and Wendy talk about four different people they know. Number the people from 1 to 4 in the order they talk about them. There is one extra person.**

☐ a classmate ☐ a co-worker ☐ a family member ☐ a neighbor ☐ a teacher

B **Listen again. Check (✓) the true sentences. Correct the false ones.**

1 ☐ Greg is graduating from middle school.
2 ☐ Eva bought a brand-new red car.
3 ☐ Mr. Landers is going to teach a new class.
4 ☐ Cathy is going to be in the school play.

3 Speaking Celebrity news

A PAIR WORK **Think of four famous people. What is some interesting news about them? Complete the chart.**

	Famous person	News
1		
2		
3		
4		

B CLASS ACTIVITY **Announce your news about the famous people to a classmate. Then close the conversation and talk to another classmate.**

C CLASS ACTIVITY **Who heard the most interesting news?**

I can announce news.
I can close a conversation.

C I was really frightened!

1 Vocabulary Verbs to describe reactions

A 🎧 **Match the words and the pictures. Then listen and check your answers.**

a amuse	c confuse	e embarrass	g frighten
b challenge	d disgust	f excite	h interest

1  ☐

2  ☐

3  ☐

4  ☐

5  ☐

6  ☐

7  ☐

8 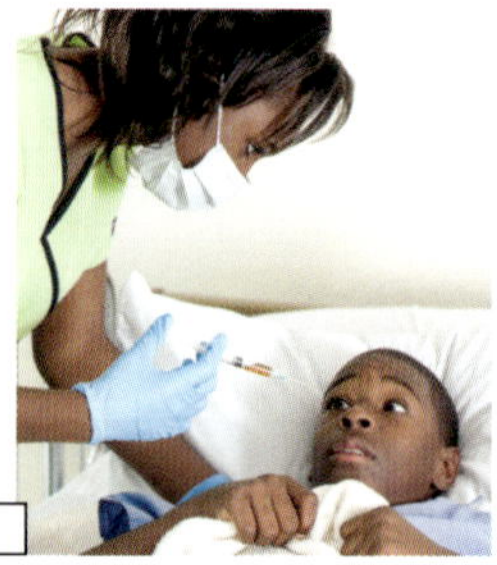 ☐

B PAIR WORK **What amuses you? Challenges you? Confuses you? Etc. Tell your partner.**

2 Conversation Around the campfire

A 🎧 **Listen to the conversation. What frightened Paul?**

David	. . . and that's what was on the floor!
Jim	Yuck! That story was disgusting!
Paul	Well, listen to this. I was watching a movie at home one night when I heard a strange noise outside the window.
David	What did you do?
Paul	I was really frightened! I was watching a horror movie, *and* I was sitting in the dark. Anyway, I walked to the window, opened the curtains, and saw a face!
Jim	No way! That's frightening!
Paul	Not really. It was just my roommate.
David	Your roommate?
Paul	Yeah. Unfortunately, he lost his key and couldn't get in the house. He was really embarrassed!

B 🎧 **Listen to the rest of the conversation. How did Paul's roommate react?**

3 Grammar Participial adjectives

Use present participles (-ing) to describe someone or something that causes a reaction.	*Use past participles (-ed) to describe a person's reaction to someone or something.*
That story was **disgusting**.	I was **disgusted** by that story.
The noise was really **frightening**.	I was really **frightened** by the noise.
His actions were really **embarrassing**.	He was really **embarrassed**.

Circle the correct words. Then compare with a partner.

1 This short story is very (**challenging**) / **challenged**. There's a lot of difficult vocabulary.
2 I'm really **exciting** / **excited** to hear about your trip. Tell me all about it!
3 I liked your story, but I'm **confusing** / **confused** by the ending. Can you explain it?
4 I think my neighbor's stories about her life are very **amusing** / **amused**.
5 I never feel **frightening** / **frightened** when people tell me ghost stories.
6 That joke wasn't funny at all. It was **disgusting** / **disgusted**.
7 That movie was **boring** / **bored**. It wasn't **interesting** / **interested** at all.
8 I'm **surprising** / **surprised** you were **embarrassing** / **embarrassed** by my story.

4 Listening Is that really true?

A Listen to Mark's story. Check (✓) the two adjectives that best describe it.

☐ challenging ☐ frightening ☐ disgusting ☐ amusing

B Listen again. Answer the questions.

1 What are Mark and his friend doing in the tent? ____________
2 What did they first hear outside the tent? ____________
3 What did Mark's friend want to do? ____________
4 What did the voice outside the tent say? ____________

5 Speaking My own experience

A Think about your own experiences. Choose one of the topics from the list below. Then take notes to prepare to talk about it.

an exciting day	a frightening experience
a confusing moment	an amusing situation
a challenging situation	an interesting conversation

B PAIR WORK Tell your partner about your experience. Ask and answer questions for more information.

6 Keep talking!

Go to page 126 for more practice.

I can tell personal stories.

D How embarrassing!

1 Reading

A How do you react when you feel embarrassed? Do you turn red? Do you get angry if people laugh at you?

B Read the article. Where did each person's embarrassing moment happen?

STUDENT TIMES Home | Metro | Sports | Opinions | Arts | Photos | Videos | Search

Embarrassing Experiences

By Jack Preston

Last week, *Student Times* reporter Jack Preston asked students, "What's the most embarrassing experience you've ever had?" Here are five of his favorite responses.

This happened at work a few years ago. I was on an elevator, and a man got on that I didn't know. He asked, "How are you?" I answered, "Pretty good." Then he asked, "What's new?" and I said, "Nothing much." Finally, he turned and said, "Do you mind?" He was on his cell phone! I was so embarrassed! ☐ – ***Susan***

I sing all the time. One time, a few years ago, I was singing in the shower when my sister came into the bathroom and recorded me! Later, we were driving, and my sister put on some music. ☐ It was me! I was really embarrassed and turned bright red. – ***Becky***

I fell asleep in math class once. I closed my eyes for a second, and the next thing I remember is my teacher's voice. He was asking me a question. When I didn't answer, he walked over to my desk. He asked the question again. ☐ – ***Alex***

My friend's parents had a birthday party for her at their new house last year. They had these glass doors that went out to the backyard. We were all outside, and I had to use the restroom. So I was running to the house and then – BAM! I hit the glass doors. I was really confused for a minute. I thought they were open, but they were closed! ☐ – ***Anita***

When I was in middle school, I bought this cool new sweater. I wore it to a school dance the next evening, and everyone laughed at me when I came in. The sweater was inside out! So I went into the restroom to change and came back out. ☐ Everyone laughed at me again. – ***Evan***

C Read the article again. Write the numbers of the missing sentences in the correct paragraphs.

1 Luckily, I knew the answer.
2 Fortunately, the doors opened, and I got off.
3 Unfortunately, it was now on backwards!
4 Suddenly, she started to laugh.
5 Amazingly, I wasn't hurt at all.

D PAIR WORK Whose story do you think is the most embarrassing? Discuss your ideas.

2 Writing An embarrassing moment

A Think of an embarrassing moment that happened to you or someone you know. Answer the questions.

- When did it happen? ____________
- Where did it happen? ____________
- Who was there? ____________
- Why was it embarrassing? ____________

B Write a description of an embarrassing moment that happened to you or someone you know. Use the model and your answers in Part A to help you.

Embarrassed at the Supermarket

When I was about six years old, I was at the supermarket with my mom. She was shopping for groceries. I wanted some candy, but my mom didn't want to buy me any. So, when my mother wasn't looking, I took some candy and put it into the cart. The problem was that I put the candy into the wrong cart . . .

C CLASS ACTIVITY Post your papers around the classroom. Then read the stories and rate them from 1 (very embarrassing) to 4 (not embarrassing at all). Which stories are the most embarrassing?

3 Speaking It happened to me!

A Imagine you are the person in one of these pictures. Take notes to prepare to tell the story.

B GROUP WORK Tell your stories. Ask and answer questions for more information.

A: I was having dinner with my wife. We were at a restaurant and I accidentally went into the ladies' restroom instead of the men's restroom.

B: Oh, no! What did you do?

I can describe embarrassing moments. ✓

Wrap-up

1 Quick pair review

Lesson A Brainstorm!

Make a list of sentence adverbs. How many do you know? You have one minute.

Lesson B Do you remember?

Complete the expressions with the correct words to announce news and close a conversation. You have one minute.

1 Did you hear ________________?
2 You'll ________________ what happened!
3 Guess ________________!
4 Listen, I've ________________ run!
5 Hey, I need to ________________.
6 Sorry, I ________________ to go.

Lesson C Test your partner!

Say four present or past participles. Can your partner use them correctly in a sentence? Take turns. You have two minutes.

A: *Disgusting.*

B: *In my opinion, hamburgers are disgusting!*

Lesson D Find out!

What are two things both you and your partner do when you are embarrassed? You have one minute.

A: *When I'm embarrassed, I laugh a lot. Do you?*

B: *No, I don't. I turn red, though. Do you?*

A: *Yes, my cheeks turn red, too!*

2 In the real world

Go online and find an embarrassing, interesting, or amusing story in English about a famous person. Then write about it.

Beyoncé's Embarrassing Moment

Beyoncé had an embarrassing experience at a concert. She was walking down the stairs on stage when she tripped and fell. Luckily, she didn't get hurt. Actually, she got up and continued to sing! . . .

3 Style and fashion

Lesson A
- Fashion statements
- *Used to*

Lesson B
- Asking where things are
- Asking for an alternative

Lesson C
- Clothing styles
- Defining relative clauses

Lesson D
- Reading: "Dress to Impress"
- Writing: Class survey

Warm Up

A Describe the pictures. What are the people doing?

B Which styles do you like? Which don't you like? Why?

A Fashion trends

1 Vocabulary Fashion statements

A Complete the chart with the correct words. Then listen and check your answers.

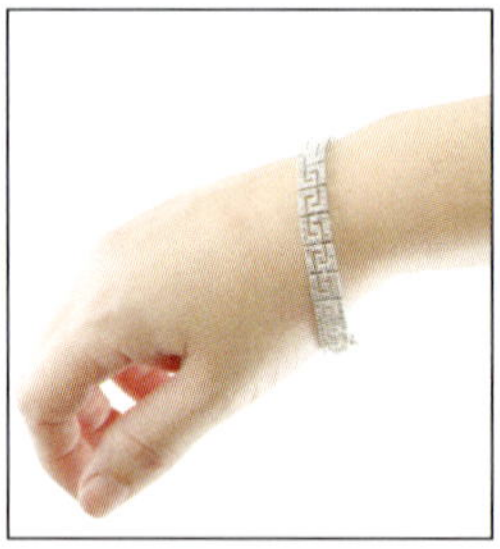
a bracelet

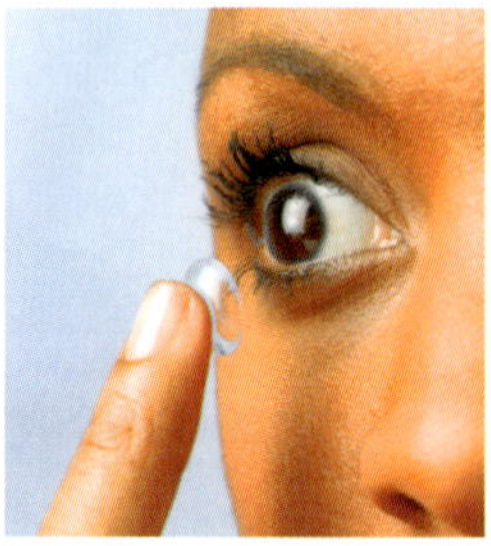
contact lenses

dyed hair

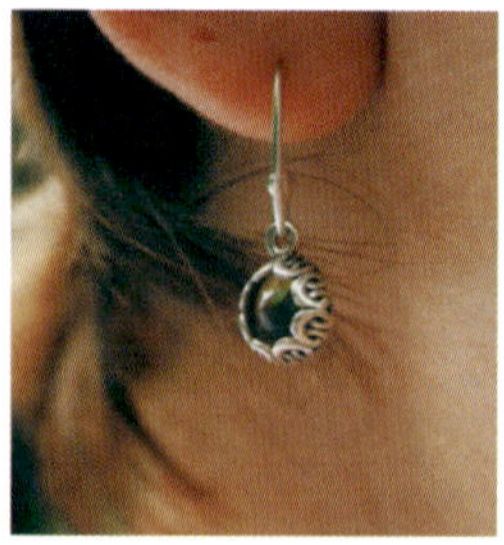
earrings

glasses

high heels

a leather jacket

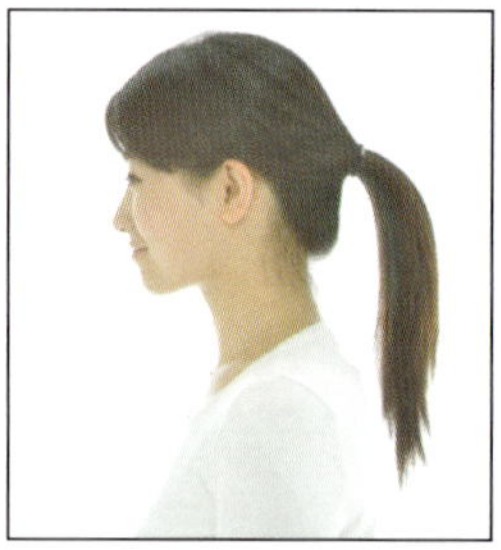
a ponytail

sandals

a uniform

Shoes	Clothing	Eyewear	Hairstyles	Jewelry

B PAIR WORK Which things in Part A do you wear or have? Tell your partner.

2 Language in context Fashion history

A Read about three fashions from the past. Who wore each fashion?

Togas Two thousand years ago, Roman men used to wear sandals and a long piece of clothing called a toga.

Wigs In the seventeenth and eighteenth centuries, rich men and women in England and France used to wear long wigs. Some of the wigs had ponytails.

Leather jackets In the 1950s, many American men used to wear leather jackets with jeans. Before that time, most teenagers didn't use to wear jeans.

B Do people still wear the fashions from Part A today? If so, how are they similar or different?

3 Grammar Used to

Used to refers to something that was true in the past but isn't anymore or something that happened regularly in the past but doesn't anymore.

I **used to** have a black leather jacket.

Men and women in England and France **used to** wear long wigs.

Did you **use to** dye your hair?
Yes, I **used to** dye my hair all the time, but I don't dye it anymore.
No, I **didn't use to** dye my hair, but I do now.

A Write sentences with *used to* (✓) or *didn't use to* (✗). Then compare with a partner.

1 Max / (✓) dye his hair black — Max used to dye his hair black.
2 Carly / (✗) wear a uniform to school ____________
3 Tina and I / (✓) have ponytails ____________
4 Britney / (✓) wear the same bracelet every day ____________
5 Roberto and Ana / (✗) wear glasses ____________
6 Kendra /(✗) like leather skirts ____________

B PAIR WORK Complete the sentences with true information. Tell your partner.

1 I used to ____________ as a kid, but I don't now.
2 I didn't use to ____________, but some of my friends did.
3 Lots of people used to ____________, but they don't now.

4 Pronunciation Used to and use to

Listen and repeat. Notice how *used to* and *use to* sound the same.

/yustə/
I **used to** wear a uniform.

/yustə/
I didn't **use to** dye my hair, but I do now.

5 Speaking Past and present

A PAIR WORK Read the list. Add two more questions about style and fashion. Then interview your partner. Take notes.

- What kind of clothing did you use to wear?
- What kind of hairstyles did you use to have?
- What's something you didn't use to wear but do now?
- ____________
- ____________

B PAIR WORK Tell another classmate any interesting information about your partner's style and fashion.

6 Keep talking!

Student A go to page 127 and Student B go to page 128 for more practice.

I can ask about and describe past fashions.

B Does this come in . . . ?

1 Interactions Shopping questions

A Where do you like to shop for clothes? What kinds of clothes do you like?

B Listen to the conversations. What size does Jenny want? Then practice the conversations.

Jenny	Excuse me.
Salesclerk 1	Yes?
Jenny	Where are the raincoats?
Salesclerk 1	They're on the second floor, in Outerwear.
Jenny	Thank you.

Jenny	Excuse me.
Salesclerk 2	Can I help you?
Jenny	Yes. Does this come in a medium?
Salesclerk 2	I believe so. Let's see. . . Yes, here you go.
Jenny	Thank you.
Salesclerk 2	If you want to try it on, the fitting rooms are over there.

C Read the expressions below. Complete each box with a similar expression from the conversations. Then listen and check your answers.

Asking where things are

____

Where can I find the . . . ?

Could you tell me where the . . . are?

Asking for an alternative

____

Do you have this in . . . ?

Can I get this in . . . ?

D PAIR WORK Have conversations like the ones in Part B. Use these items.

2 Listening Shopping for clothes

A Listen to four customers shopping in a clothing store. Number the items they discuss from 1 to 4. There are two extra items.

 ☐
 ☐
 ☐
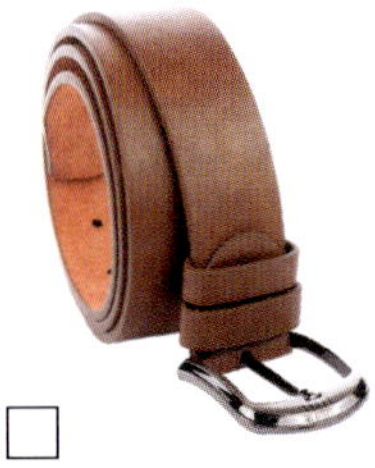 ☐
 ☐
 ☐

B Listen again. Does each customer ask the salesclerk for the location or an alternative of the item? Write L (location) or A (alternative).

1 ______ 2 ______ 3 ______ 4 ______

3 Speaking In a department store

GROUP WORK Role-play the situation. Then change roles.

Student A: You are a salesclerk in a department store. Student B is shopping for a particular item. Direct Student B to the correct section of the store. Use the picture to help you.

Student B: You are shopping in a department store. Students A and C are salesclerks. Ask Student A where a particular clothing item is. Then ask Student C for a different item.

Student C: You are a salesclerk in a department store. Student B is shopping for a particular item in your section of the store. Help Student B get a different item.

A: *Good afternoon. Can I help you?*

B: *Yes. Where can I find women's shoes?*

A: *On the second floor, in Footwear.*

I can ask where something is in a store.

I can ask for a specific product.

C The latest look

1 Vocabulary Clothing styles

A Write the correct adjectives to describe the clothing. Then listen and check your answers.

fashionable
✓ flashy
glamorous
old-fashioned

1 flashy
2 ____________
3 ____________
4 ____________

1

2

3

4

retro
tacky
trendy
✓ weird

5 weird
6 ____________
7 ____________
8 ____________

5

6

7

8

B PAIR WORK Which styles do you like? Which don't you like? Why? Tell your partner.

2 Conversation People-watching

A Listen to the conversation. What does Ryan think of the man's tie?

Ryan Look at that woman's jacket!
Jill Wow! It's pretty flashy. I definitely think she's someone who likes to stand out in a crowd.
Ryan I know what you mean. I like clothes which don't attract a lot of attention.
Jill Really?
Ryan Yeah. I usually shop for clothes that are simple and inexpensive. Hey, check out that guy's tie. Talk about old-fashioned!
Jill Do you think so? Actually, I think it's pretty fashionable. It's kind of retro.
Ryan Well, I'd never wear anything like that.

B Listen to the rest of the conversation. How does Jill describe her style?

3 Grammar Defining relative clauses

Defining relative clauses specify which or what kind of people or things you are describing.

Use that *or* who *for people.*

I'm a person **that** loves flashy clothes.

She's someone **who** likes to stand out in a crowd.

Use that *or* which *for things.*

I shop for clothes **that** are simple and inexpensive.

He likes clothes **which** don't attract a lot of attention.

A Complete each sentence with *that*, *who*, or *which*. Then compare with a partner.

1 I prefer salesclerks ________ are honest with me.
2 I'm the kind of person ________ rarely follows fashion.
3 I hardly ever wear clothes ________ are trendy.
4 I know someone ________ loves expensive clothes.
5 Some of my friends wear stuff ________ is a little too weird.
6 I usually buy clothes ________ are on sale.
7 I'm someone ________ likes reading fashion magazines.
8 I buy shoes ________ go with lots of different clothing.

B PAIR WORK Make the sentences in Part A true for you. Tell your partner.

A: *I prefer salesclerks who don't say anything. I know what looks good on me.*

B: *Not me. I need all the help I can get!*

4 Speaking Thoughts on fashion

A Complete the sentences with your own ideas.

1 I really don't like clothes that are ________ .
2 ________ is a word which describes my personal style.
3 When shopping, I like friends who ________ .
4 ________ is a person who always looks fashionable.
5 I think ________ is a color that looks good on me.
6 A ________ is something that I never wear.
7 ________ is a designer who's very popular now.

B GROUP WORK Compare your ideas. Ask and answer questions for more information.

A: *I really don't like clothes that are expensive.*

B: *Really? I only like expensive clothes!*

C: *I like clothes that are comfortable.*

5 Keep talking!

Go to page 129 for more practice.

I can express opinions about style and fashion.

D Views on fashion

1 Reading

A What's in style these days? Do you like the current fashions for men and women?

B Read the article. Do you find any of the information surprising?

Dress to Impress

Image is important to many people, but what do men and women really think of each other's fashion choices? What do people actually think looks good on the opposite sex? Are you dressing to impress your target audience? What are some clothing items that you should invest in to get someone's attention?

Fashion styles like "artsy," for the more creative crowd, or vintage, for a touch of the past, or even fancy "chic" clothing may show a little of your personality. But it doesn't always mean that the person you may be trying to impress ***will be*** impressed.

It may be simpler than you think! Women generally like men that look like they have made an effort. As for men, they seem to be the opposite! Here is what most men and women say that they prefer:

WHAT WOMEN LIKE IN MEN'S FASHION

- A well-fitted pair of jeans
- A nice watch
- One item that is cool and funky, like a hat or unusual pair of shoes
- Blue or pink shirts
- Glasses

WHAT MEN LIKE IN WOMEN'S FASHION

- Very little makeup or none at all
- A chic pair of high heels
- A flowery summer dress
- Long hair
- Glasses

C Read the article again. Are the sentences true or false? Write T (true) or F (false).

1 Most women like to wear well-fitted jeans with a blue shirt. ______
2 Both men and women like it when the other wears glasses. ______
3 You have to dress very chic if you want to attract a man. ______
4 Guys often think "less is more" for a woman. ______
5 Many guys like it when a woman wears high heels. ______
6 Most guys think women look nice with long hair. ______

D PAIR WORK Do you agree with the information in the article? Why or why not? Discuss your ideas.

2 Listening An interview with Eduardo

A Listen to an interview with Eduardo, a fashion designer. Number the questions from 1 to 5 in the order you hear them. Write the numbers in the boxes.

- ☐ Are high heels old-fashioned? ______
- ☐ Should belts and shoes be the same color? ______
- ☐ Does black go with everything? ______
- ☐ Is it OK for men to wear earrings? ______
- ☐ Can guys wear pink? ______

B Listen again. How does Eduardo answer each question? Write Y (yes) or N (no) on each line.

C Do you agree with Eduardo's opinions? Why or why not?

3 Writing and speaking Class survey

A GROUP WORK Create a survey with four questions about fashion and style. Use the topics below or your own ideas.

cool places to shop	popular colors
current clothing styles	the latest gadgets
current hairstyles	trendy accessories
popular brands	unpopular colors

Fashion Survey

1. *What color is popular right now?*
2. *What's the most popular brand of jeans?*
3. *Where is a cool place to buy jewelry?*
4. *What gadget does everyone want now?*

B CLASS ACTIVITY Ask and answer the questions in your surveys. Take notes.

C GROUP WORK Share and summarize the results.

Our Class Survey Results

Most people think blue is popular right now. Red was second and green was third. Only a few people think black, orange, or purple are popular. Only one person thinks yellow is popular.

The most popular brand of jeans is Sacco. A lot of people have these. Next was a brand called Durango. These were the only two brands that people mentioned.

Over half of the people in class think Glitter is a cool place to buy jewelry. Some people think the best place to buy jewelry is from people who sell it on the street. Two people . . .

D CLASS ACTIVITY Share your most interesting results. Do you agree with the answers you heard? Give your own opinions.

I can ask and talk about current fashions.

Wrap-up

1 Quick pair review

Lesson A Do you remember?

Cross out the word that doesn't belong. Then write the category. You have two minutes.

1	______	high heels	sandals	glasses
2	______	a bracelet	contact lenses	earrings
3	______	dyed hair	a uniform	a ponytail
4	______	a uniform	high heels	a leather jacket
5	______	glasses	contact lenses	earrings

Lesson B Brainstorm!

Make a list of three ways to ask where something is and three ways to ask for an alternative. You have two minutes.

Lesson C Test your partner!

Say each pair of sentences. Can your partner make them into one sentence with *which* or *who*? You have two minutes.

Student A

1 I'm a trendy person. I don't like old-fashioned clothes.
2 I usually wear glasses. They aren't glamorous.
3 Julie shops for stuff. It is affordable.

Student B

1 I usually wear hats. They are weird.
2 I know someone. She likes flashy bracelets.
3 Kyle is a guy. He wears tacky clothes.

A: I'm a trendy person. I don't like old-fashioned clothes.

B: I'm a trendy person who doesn't like old-fashioned clothes.

Lesson D Find out!

What are two colors that both you and your partner think are good for women to wear? What are two colors you both think are good for guys to wear? You have two minutes.

2 In the real world

What clothes used to be trendy? Go online and find examples of trendy clothes from one decade in the past. Then write about them.

1950s	1960s	1970s	1980s	1990s

Trends in the 1950s

Long dresses used to be popular in the 1950s. Poodle skirts used to be trendy, too. Women used to . . .

4 Interesting lives

Lesson A
- Experiences
- Present perfect

Lesson B
- Checking meaning
- Clarifying meaning

Lesson C
- Fun things to do
- Present perfect vs. simple past

Lesson D
- Reading "The Life of an Astronaut"
- Writing: Interesting people, places, or things

Warm Up

A Describe the pictures. What are the people doing?

B Check (✓) the two most interesting activities. Have you ever done them? If not, would you like to try them?

A Have you ever been on TV?

1 Vocabulary Experiences

A Complete the phrases with the correct words. Then listen and check your answers.

an award	a famous person	on TV	to a new city
a bone	✓in a play	seasick	your phone

1 act in a play

2 be ______

3 break ______

4 get ______

5 lose ______

6 meet ______

7 move ______

8 win ______

B PAIR WORK **Which experiences in Part A are good to have? Which are not good to have? Discuss your ideas.**

"It's good to win an award. It's not good to get seasick."

2 Language in context A local hero

A Read Brian's group messages with some friends. Why is Brian excited?

Brian 17:02
You'll never believe what happened! I'm going to be on the TV news tonight! My first time!

Jill 17:02
You're kidding! Why?

Brian 17:03
It's a surprise. You have to watch. Have you ever been on TV?

Jill 17:03
No, I haven't. One of my friends is an actress, though, and I've seen her on TV a couple of times.

Hideo 17:03
I've never been on TV, but my sister Kumiko has been on TV lots of times. She's a TV reporter!

B What about you? Would you like to be on TV? Why or why not?

3 Grammar Present perfect

Use the present perfect to describe events or experiences that happened at an unspecified time in the past. Use have / has *and the past participle of the verb.*

Have you ever **seen** a friend on TV?
Yes, I **have**.
No, I **haven't**.

Has your sister ever **been** on TV?
Yes, she **has**.
No, she **hasn't**.

Use frequency expressions with the present perfect to give more information.

I've **never** been on TV.
My sister has been on TV **lots of times**.

A **Complete the conversations with the present perfect forms of the verbs. Then practice with a partner.**

1 A ________ you ever ________ (be) to another country?
B Yes, I ________ . I ________ (be) to Brazil.

2 A ________ you ever ________ (eat) sushi?
B Yes, I ________ . I ________ (have) it many times.

3 A ________ you ever ________ (lose) your wallet?
B No, I ________. Luckily, I ________ never ________ (lose) it.

4 A ________ your best friend ever ________ (call) you in the middle of the night?
B No, she ________ . But I ________ (do) that to her once or twice!

B PAIR WORK **Ask and answer the questions in Part A. Answer with your own information.**

Regular past participles

act → acted
chat → chatted
try → tried

Irregular past participles

be → been
break → broken
do → done
eat → eaten
go → gone
have → had
lose → lost
meet → met
see → seen
win → won

Turn to page 151 for a list of more past participles.

4 Speaking Yes, I have!

A **Complete the questions with your own ideas. Then check (✓) the things you've done, and write down how often you've done them.**

Have you ever . . . ?	Me		Name ________		Name ________	
eaten ________	☐		☐		☐	
been ________	☐		☐		☐	
seen ________	☐		☐		☐	
had ________	☐		☐		☐	
won ________	☐		☐		☐	
met ________	☐		☐		☐	

B GROUP WORK **Interview two classmates. Complete the chart with their answers. Who has had similar experiences?**

5 Keep talking!

Go to page 130 for more practice.

I can ask and talk about life experiences.

3 What I mean is...

1 Interactions Checking and clarifying meaning

A How often do you eat out? Do you ever cook at home? Do you ever order takeout?

B Listen to the conversation. How often does Sam eat out? Then practice the conversation.

Elena: I'm getting hungry.
Sam: Me, too.
Elena: Hey, Sam, there's a great Mexican restaurant near the school. Have you ever tried it?
Sam: No, I haven't. Actually, I don't eat in restaurants.
Elena: Really? Are you saying you never go to restaurants?
Sam: Well, no, not *never*. I mean I just don't eat out very often.
Elena: Why not?
Sam: I'm allergic to certain foods, like peanuts. If I eat them, my skin gets red and itchy.
Elena: That sounds awful!
Sam: It is!

C Read the expressions below. Complete each box with a similar expression from the conversation. Then listen and check your answers.

Checking meaning	Clarifying meaning
______	______
Do you mean . . .?	What I mean is, . . .
Does that mean . . .?	What I'm saying is, . . .

D Number the sentences in the conversation from 1 to 7. Then practice with a partner.

____ A: What? Do you mean you never eat pizza?
____ A: I see. So, when can I come over for homemade pizza?
__1__ A: I feel a little hungry.
____ A: Have you ever been to Pizza Palace? We can go there.
____ B: So do I.
____ B: No, not *never*. What I mean is, I usually make it myself.
____ B: Actually, I never go to fast-food places.

2 Pronunciation Contrastive stress in responses

A 🎧 **Listen and repeat. Notice how the stressed words emphasize contrast.**

Are you saying you never go to restaurants?

Well, not **never**. I mean I just don't eat out **very often**.

B PAIR WORK **Practice the conversation in Exercise 1D again. Stress words to emphasize contrast.**

3 Listening Why not?

A 🎧 **Listen to four conversations about habits and preferences. Correct the false information.**

1 Danielle ~~often~~ never goes to hair salons.
2 Todd loves going to the beach.
3 Jessica always walks to school.
4 Mitch never streams movies.

B 🎧 **Listen again. How do the people explain their habits and preferences? Check (✓) the correct answers.**

1 Danielle's explanation:
- ☐ She finds it too expensive.
- ☐ Her sister cuts her hair.
- ☐ She cuts her own hair.

2 Todd's explanation:
- ☐ It's not easy to get there.
- ☐ He doesn't know how to swim.
- ☐ He doesn't like to be in the sun.

3 Jessica's explanation:
- ☐ The school is only five minutes away.
- ☐ She doesn't have a driver's license.
- ☐ She prefers to walk for the exercise.

4 Mitch's explanation:
- ☐ The movie theater is too far away.
- ☐ He thinks tickets are too expensive.
- ☐ He prefers to stream movies at home.

4 Speaking Unusual habits

A 🎧 **Write four statements about any unusual or interesting habits and behaviors you have. Use the questions to help you, or think of your own ideas.**

- Is there a food you eat all the time?
- Is there a place you never go?
- Is there someone you talk to every day?
- Is there something you never do?
- Is there an expression you say all the time?

1 ______________________ 3 ______________________

2 ______________________ 4 ______________________

B PAIR WORK **Tell your partner about each habit or behavior. Your partner checks the meaning, and you clarify it. Take turns.**

A: *I eat chocolate all the time.*

B: *Does that mean you eat it every day?*

A: *Well, no, not every day. I mean I have chocolate several times a week.*

I can check and clarify meaning. ✓

C Life experiences

1 Vocabulary Fun things to do

A Match the phrases and the pictures. Then listen and check your answers.

a	climb a mountain	c	go camping	e	go whale-watching	g	try an exotic food
b	eat in a fancy restaurant	d	go to a spa	f	ride a roller coaster	h	try an extreme sport

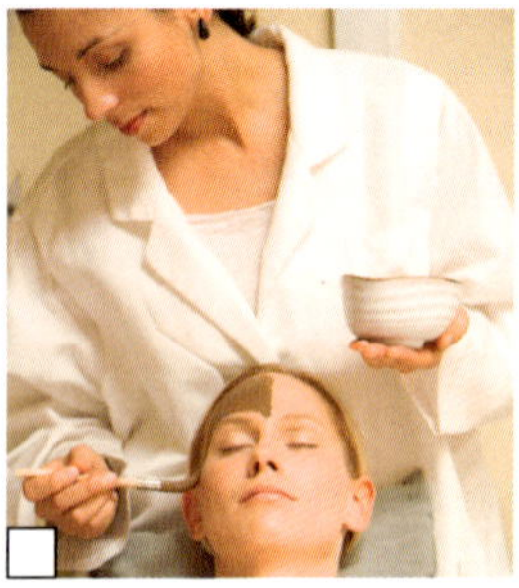
1 ☐

2 ☐

3 ☐

4 ☐

5 ☐

6 ☐

7 ☐

8 ☐

B PAIR WORK **Have you ever done the fun things in Part A? Tell your partner.**

2 Conversation A fancy restaurant

A Listen to the conversation. Do you think Alice will order frog legs?

Alice: Wow! This place is nice!

Emma: Have you ever eaten in a fancy restaurant before?

Alice: Yes, I have. I've eaten in a few expensive restaurants, but this place is amazing.

Emma: You can try a lot of exotic food here, and all of their dishes are excellent. Oh, look. Tonight's special is frog legs.

Alice: Frog legs? Umm, I don't know. . . .

Emma: Have you ever tried them?

Alice: No, I haven't. But my brother tried them once a few years ago.

Emma: Did he like them?

Alice: I don't think so. He got sick later that night.

B Listen to the rest of the conversation. What do Alice and Emma order?

3 Grammar Present perfect vs. simple past

Use the present perfect to describe events or experiences at an unspecified time in the past.

Have you ever **eaten** in a fancy restaurant?
Yes, I **have**. I**'ve eaten** in a few expensive restaurants.

Use the simple past to describe events or experiences that happened at a specific time in the past.

Have you ever tried frog legs?
No, I haven't. But my brother **tried** them once **a few years ago**.

Did he **like** them?
I don't think so. He **got** sick later **that night**.

A **Complete the conversations with the present perfect or simple past forms of the verbs. Then practice with a partner.**

1 A ________ you ever ________ (see) a whale?
B No, I ________. But I ________ always ________ (want) to.

2 A ________ you ________ (do) anything fun last weekend?
B Yes, I ________. I ________ (go) camping with my sister.

3 A ________ you ever ________ (eat) in a fancy restaurant?
B Yes, I ________. I ________ (go) to Lucia's last year.

4 A What extreme sports ________ you ________ (try)?
B I ________ (not / try) any. But my sister ________ (go) skydiving once!

5 A What ________ you ________ (do) on your last vacation?
B My friend and I ________ (go) to a spa.

B PAIR WORK **Ask and answer the questions in Part A. Answer with your own information.**

4 Speaking Is that true?

A **Write two true sentences and one false sentence about interesting life experiences you've had.**

1 ________
2 ________
3 ________

B GROUP WORK **Share your sentences. Your group asks you questions and guesses the false sentence. Take turns.**

A: *I've been to a wrestling match.*
B: *Really? Who did you go with?*

5 Keep talking!

Go to page 131 for more practice.

I can describe details of my experiences.

D What a life!

1 Reading

A What do you think an astronaut's life is like? What do people need to do or know to become astronauts?

B Read the interview. According to Dr. Pettit, what's the most exciting thing he's experienced?

The life of an ASTRONAUT

Dr. Donald Pettit is a NASA astronaut.

Interviewer: I'm sure people ask you this question all of the time, Dr. Pettit, but I have to ask it: Have you ever been to space?

Dr. Pettit: Yes, I have. I was a crew member of *Expedition 6*, and I spent five and a half months at the International Space Station. We call it the ISS.

Interviewer: How many times have you gone up on the space shuttle?

Dr. Pettit: I've ridden the space shuttle to the ISS twice.

Interviewer: And what was the best part about being in space?

Dr. Pettit: Being able to float. It was the worst part, too.

Interviewer: Have you visited any other interesting places while working for NASA?

Dr. Pettit: Well, I lived in Russia for about two years while I was training to fly to the ISS. I've also been to Antarctica.

Interviewer: Not many people can say that! I understand that you like to work with tools. Have you ever invented anything?

Dr. Pettit: Yes. During my second trip into space, I made a special coffee cup so we could drink in space, much like we do here on Earth. I just couldn't get used to drinking coffee out of a small bag through a straw!

Interviewer: I don't think I could get used to that, either. But why did you have to drink coffee that way before?

Dr. Pettit: Without the bag or my special cup, the coffee floats in space, too.

Interviewer: Of course! Well, you've accomplished so much, Dr. Pettit. Considering all of it, what's the most exciting thing that you've experienced?

Dr. Pettit: Seeing the birth of my twin boys.

Interviewer: Wow, what a life! Thanks so much for sharing, Dr. Pettit.

C Read the interview again. What things has Dr. Pettit done? Check (✓) the correct answers.

- ☐ walked on the moon
- ☐ been to the ISS
- ☐ ridden the space shuttle
- ☐ traveled to Antarctica
- ☐ had twin daughters
- ☐ invented something

D PAIR WORK Would you like to travel to space? Why or why not? What would be the most interesting thing about it? Discuss your ideas.

2 Listening A memorable life

A Listen to Leo ask his grandmother about her life. Number the questions from 1 to 5 in the order that you hear them.

☐ When did you meet Grandpa? ____________________

☐ What's something interesting you've done? ____________________

☐ Where else have you lived? ____________________

☐ Where were you born? ____________________

☐ Have you been back? ____________________

B Listen again. Write the grandmother's answers to the questions in Part A.

3 Writing and speaking Interesting people, places, or things

A Choose one of the topics. Answer the questions.

Topics	Questions
A close friend I've had	Who is your friend? How exactly did you meet? Is this person your friend now? Why or why not?
A special place I've been	Where is this place? What made this place so special? Have you ever been back? Why or why not?
An interesting thing I've done	What did you do? How did you feel after doing it? Would you like to do it again? Why or why not?

B Write a paragraph about your topic. Use the model and your answers in Part A to help you.

My Friend Lucas

I've had had several good friends, but one that was very special to me was my friend Lucas. He moved into the house next door when I was eight. We became good friends. We walked to school together and always played together at his house. He had a great bike, and I used to ride it. He moved to another city after a year. I've tried to find him online, but haven't had any luck. I . . .

C PAIR WORK Read your partner's paragraph. Write five questions to get more information.

D PAIR WORK Ask and answer your questions.

"So, tell me, why did you become friends?"

I can ask and talk about a memorable experience.

Wrap-up

1 Quick pair review

Lesson A Find out!

What is one place both you and your partner have been? One food you both have tried? One movie you both have seen? You have two minutes.

A: *I've been to the art museum downtown. Have you?*

B: *No, I haven't. I've been to our university library. Have you?*

A: *Yes, I have.*

Lesson B Do you remember?

What can you say to clarify meaning? Check (✓) your answers. You have one minute.

- ☐ What I mean is, . . .
- ☐ What time is . . . ?
- ☐ What I'm saying is, . . .
- ☐ I didn't use to . . .
- ☐ I mean . . .
- ☐ I used to go . . .

Lesson C Brainstorm!

Imagine you and your partner are going on vacation together. Make a list of eight fun things to do on your trip. You have two minutes.

Lesson D Guess!

Describe a memorable experience you've had, but don't say where it was. Can your partner guess where you were? You have two minutes.

2 In the real world

What do you think would be a memorable vacation? Find information in English online or in a travel magazine about one place. Then write about it.

A Vacation in Hawaii

Hawaii is a good place for a vacation. I've always wanted to go whale-watching, and I read that you can see whales in the Pacific Ocean from December to early May. The best places to see them are Maui, Molokai, and Lanai.

I've also read about Haleakala National Park in Hawaii. A lot of people climb Mount Haleakala. I've seen pictures of it. It looks really beautiful. The weather is usually . . .

5 Our world

Lesson A
- Human-made wonders
- Comparisons with adjectives and nouns

Lesson B
- Expressing disbelief
- Saying you don't know

Lesson C
- Geographical features
- Superlatives with adjectives and nouns

Lesson D
- Reading "Seven Wonders of the Natural World"
- Writing: A natural wonder

☐ Burj Khalifa – the U.A.E.

☐ Chichén Itzá – Mexico

☐ Icehotel – Sweden

☐ Cinque Terre – Italy

☐ Yellowstone National Park – the U.S.A.

☐ Kinkaku-ji Temple – Japan

Warm Up

A Look at the pictures. Rank the places you would like to visit from 1 (the most) to 6 (the least).

B Why do you want to visit your top three places?

A Older, taller, and more famous

1 Vocabulary Human-made wonders

A 🎧 **Label the pictures with the correct words. Then listen and check your answers.**

bridge	plaza	stadium	tower
canal	skyscraper	subway system	tunnel

1 ______________

2 ______________

3 ______________

4 ______________

5 ______________

6 ______________

7 ______________

8 ______________

B PAIR WORK **Can you name a famous example for each word? Tell your partner.**

"The Panama Canal is very famous."

2 Language in context Two amazing views

A 🎧 **Read the question posted on a website for visitors to New York City. Which view does the site recommend?**

Which is better, the view from the top of the Empire State Building or Rockefeller Center?

Good question! The Empire State Building is older, taller, and more famous than Rockefeller Center, so it gets more visitors. But the lines to get to the top of Rockefeller Center aren't as long as the lines at the Empire State Building. Tickets are more expensive, but I think the view is better. You can see Central Park on one side and the Empire State Building on the other!

B **What about you? Where can you go in your town or city for a great view? Have you ever been there?**

3 Grammar Comparisons with adjectives and nouns

Use the -er *ending or* more . . . than *with adjectives to make comparisons.*
The Empire State Building is **older**, **taller**, and **more famous than** Rockefeller Center.

You can also use not as . . . as *to make comparisons with adjectives.*
The lines at Rockefeller Center are**n't as long as** the lines at the Empire State Building.
Tickets to the Empire State Building are**n't as expensive as** tickets to Rockefeller Center.

Use more . . . than *to make comparisons with nouns.*
The Empire State Building gets **more visitors than** Rockefeller Center.
Rockefeller Center has **more observation space than** the Empire State Building.

A Read the information about the Maracanã Stadium and Nissan Stadium. Make comparisons with the adjectives and nouns below. Then compare with a partner.

Maracanã Stadium, Brazil

Year opened: 1950
Seating capacity: 87,101 people
Field size: 88,802 square feet
Height: 105 feet
Number of tiers: 1
Length of construction: 1 year and 10 months

Nissan Stadium, Japan

Year opened: 1998
Seating capacity: 72,327 people
Field size: 82,925 square feet
Height: 170 feet
Number of tiers: 2
Length of construction: 3 years and 9 months

1 (new) Maracanã Stadium *isn't as new as Nissan Stadium*.
2 (people) Maracanã Stadium ______.
3 (big) Nissan Stadium ______.
4 (tall) Nissan Stadium ______.
5 (tiers) Maracanã Stadium ______.
6 (long) The construction of Maracanã Stadium ______.

B PAIR WORK **Which soccer stadium do you think is more crowded? Why? Discuss your ideas.**

4 Speaking Comparisons

PAIR WORK **Complete the chart with two examples of each place. Then make comparisons with the adjectives and nouns in the chart.**

Places	Example 1	Example 2	Comparisons
cities			people? / exciting?
stadiums			old? / big?
skyscrapers			tall? / modern?
universities			expensive? / students?

A: I'm sure . . . has more people than . . .
B: That's right. But I think . . . is more exciting than . . .

5 Keep talking!

Student A go to page 132 and Student B go to page 134 for more practice.

I can compare human-made structures.

B I don't believe it!

1 Interactions Interesting and unknown facts

A What are the oldest human-made structures in your country? How old are they?

B Listen to the conversation. What question can't Rachel answer? Then practice the conversation.

Rachel	This is pretty interesting. Look at this.
Keith	What's that?
Rachel	I'm looking at this website about the statues on Easter Island. It says they've found almost 900 statues.
Keith	No way!
Rachel	Yes. Most of the statues face inland. Only a few of them face the sea.
Keith	When did the Easter Islanders make them?
Rachel	Let's see. . . . About 500 to 750 years ago.
Keith	They look so heavy, don't they?
Rachel	Yes, they do.
Keith	How did they move them?
Rachel	I really don't know. But let's see if we can find out.

C Read the expressions below. Complete each box with a similar expression from the conversation. Then listen and check your answers.

Expressing disbelief

____

Seriously?

I don't believe it!

Saying you don't know

____

I have no idea.

I don't have a clue.

D PAIR WORK Continue the conversation in Part B with these questions and answers. Use the expressions in Part C.

How tall is the tallest statue?	more than 20 meters tall!
Why did they stop building them?	(say you don't know)
How far is Easter Island from Chile?	more than 3,200 kilometers!
Do you think you'll ever go there?	(say you don't know)

2 Pronunciation Intonation in tag questions

A **Listen and repeat. Notice the falling intonation in tag questions when the speaker expects the listener to agree or expects something to be true.**

The statues look so heavy, don't they? The island is beautiful, isn't it?

B **PAIR WORK** **Practice the tag questions. Pay attention to your intonation.**

1 Easter Island is part of Chile, isn't it?
2 You read that online, didn't you?
3 She wasn't sure, was she?
4 You've never been there, have you?
5 We should go there, shouldn't we?
6 They'll probably go there, won't they?

3 Listening "Manhattan of the Desert"

A **Listen to two people talk about the city of Shibam, in Yemen. Number the questions from 1 to 5 in the order you hear them.**

☐ Is it easy to get to? ____________
☐ How many people live there? ____________
☐ What's it famous for? ____________
☐ How high are the tallest buildings? ____________
☐ How old is the city? ____________

B **Listen again. Answer the questions in Part A.**

4 Speaking Did you know . . . ?

A **Make a list of three interesting facts about human-made structures.**

1. There used to be soccer games and bullfights in Plaza Mayor in Madrid, Spain.
2. More people ride the Tokyo Metro in Japan each year than any other subway system in the world.
3. The TV screen in the AT&T Stadium in Dallas, Texas, is almost 50 meters long!

B **GROUP WORK** **Share your interesting facts. Your group expresses disbelief and asks questions for more information. If you don't know the answers to their questions, say you don't know.**

A: Did you know that there used to be soccer games and bullfights in Plaza Mayor in Madrid, Spain?

B: Bullfights? Seriously? Why is it famous?

A: I don't have a clue.

C **How many questions could you answer correctly about the structures on your list? Which classmate could answer the most questions?**

I can express disbelief. ✓

I can say that I don't know something. ✓

C World geography

1 Vocabulary Geographical features

A Match the descriptions and the pictures. Then listen and check your answers.

a The largest **desert** in Asia is the Gobi Desert.
b There are about 17,000 **islands** in Indonesia.
c Siberia's Lake Baikal is the world's deepest **lake**.
d The Indian **Ocean** covers 20% of the earth's surface.
e **Rain forests** cover almost 75% of Brunei.
f China's Yangtze River is the longest **river** in Asia.
g Langtang Valley is one of the prettiest **valleys** in Nepal.
h The highest **waterfall** in India is Jog Falls.

1 ______

2 ______

3 ______

4 ______

5 ______

6 ______

7 ______

8 ______

B PAIR WORK What's another example of each geographical feature? Tell your partner.

2 Conversation Welcome to Bali.

A Listen to the conversation. When does Bali get a lot of rain?

Guide Welcome to Bali, one of the most beautiful islands in the world.
Sam It's definitely the most beautiful island I've ever visited. Is Bali the biggest island in Indonesia?
Guide No. Actually, it's one of the smallest, but it has a lot of people. The island of Java has the most people.
Sam Is that right? The weather seems pretty nice right now. Is this the best time of year to visit?
Guide Oh, yes. It's the dry season. We get the most sunshine this time of year. The wettest time is from November to April.
Sam Well, that's good. Um, what's that?
Guide Oh. It looks like rain.

B Listen to the rest of the conversation. Why is Sam visiting Bali?

3 Grammar Superlatives with adjectives and nouns

Use the -est *ending or* the most *to express the superlative with adjectives.*

The wettest time is from November to April.
Bali is **the most beautiful** island I've ever visited.
The dry season is **the best** time to visit.

Use the most *to express the superlative with nouns.*

Java has **the most people** of all the islands in Indonesia.
Bali gets **the most sunshine** in the dry season.

A Complete the conversations with the superlative forms of the adjectives. Then practice with a partner.

A I'm thinking of visiting Chile next year.
B Great! You should try to visit my hometown, Viña del Mar.
One of ____________ (popular) beaches in the country is there. It's north of Santiago.
A OK. Should I try to go to the Atacama Desert?
B Definitely. I think it's ____________ (beautiful) part of the country.
It's one of ____________ (dry) places in the world, too.
A Cool. And how about Patagonia?
B Well, that's in the south. Remember, Chile is ____________ (long) country in the world. It takes time to see it all.
A When's ____________ (good) time to visit?
B Anytime is fine. But I think ____________ (nice) time is between November and May.

The Atacama Desert, Chile

B PAIR WORK **Make true sentences about your country with the phrases below.**

the most cars	the most fun	the most rain	the most tourists

4 Speaking Tell me about it.

A GROUP WORK **Discuss your experiences in different geographical locations.**

- What's the most beautiful island you've ever seen?
- What's the coldest lake, river, or ocean you've ever swum in?
- What's the highest mountain you've ever climbed?
- What's the prettiest geographical location you've ever taken a picture of?
- What's the most amazing place you've ever walked through?

B Share your information. Who has had the most interesting experience?

5 Keep talking!

Go to page 133 for more practice.

I can ask and talk about geographical features.

D Natural wonders

1 Reading

A What do you think is the most amazing natural wonder in the world? Why?

B Read the article. What are the seven wonders, and where are they?

SEVEN WONDERS OF THE NATURAL WORLD

Here is a list of some of the most fascinating places in the world.

Located in the Himalayas on the border of Nepal and Tibet, Mount Everest is the highest mountain in the world – and one of the most dangerous to climb. But that doesn't stop people from trying to get to the top of it every year!

Over five million people visit the Grand Canyon in the U.S. state of Arizona every year. The breathtaking landscape is 445 kilometers long, 24 kilometers wide, and more than a kilometer deep!

Paricutín Volcano in Mexico is more than 300 meters high, but it used to be a flat cornfield. In 1943, people saw the earth steam and crack. It grew into a new volcano in just two years!

The Rio de Janeiro Harbor in Brazil is one of the biggest and most amazing harbors in the world. It has beautiful beaches and the famous Sugar Loaf Mountain.

Have you ever heard the crashing sound of millions of liters of water? The Zambezi River between Zambia and Zimbabwe falls 120 meters, making Victoria Falls one of the largest and loudest waterfalls on the planet.

The Great Barrier Reef is not just one colorful coral reef. It's actually almost 3,000 of them! Many plants and gorgeous tropical fish live among these reefs off the coast of Australia.

The Northern Lights are exactly what their name suggests: bright, flashing lights of amazing shapes and colors in the northern sky. The North Pole has the best view of them.

C Read the article again. Complete the sentences with the correct natural wonders.

1 ______________ has beautiful beaches.
2 ______________ is a very loud waterfall.
3 ______________ is over a kilometer deep.
4 ______________ formed in two years.
5 ______________ change in shape and color.
6 ______________ is off a country's coast.

D PAIR WORK Rank the natural wonders from 1 (most amazing) to 7 (least amazing). Then compare answers.

2 Listening The Great Barrier Reef

A Listen to a guide talk to two tourists at the Great Barrier Reef. Which statements surprise the tourists? Check (✓) the correct answers.

- [ ] The Great Barrier Reef is made up of many smaller reefs.
- [ ] You can see the reef from space.
- [ ] You can see turtles near the reef.
- [ ] Global warming can make the coral appear white.

B Listen again. Answer the questions.

1. How many kinds of coral are there? ______
2. How does the coral look on TV? ______
3. What's the weather like today? ______
4. What does the guide say to do? ______

3 Writing A natural wonder

A Think of a natural wonder in your country.

- Where is it? ______
- What does it look like? ______
- What can you do there? ______
- When's a good time to go there? ______

B Write a paragraph about the natural wonder. Use the model and your answers in Part A to help you.

A Wonderful Mountain

Mount Toubkal is the highest mountain in Morocco, and one of the prettiest. The most popular time to visit is the summer. Many people climb the mountain, and you can hike it in two days. To me, the most interesting time to visit is the winter because you can ski. This is surprising to many people. . . .

C GROUP WORK Share your paragraphs. Can anyone add more information?

4 Speaking Seven wonders of my country

A PAIR WORK Make a list of the top seven natural or human-made wonders in your country. Why are they wonderful? Take notes.

B CLASS ACTIVITY Share your lists and reasons. Then vote on the top seven wonders to create one list.

I can describe natural wonders in my country.

Wrap-up

1 Quick pair review

Lesson A Brainstorm!

Make a list of human-made wonders. How many do you know? You have one minute.

Lesson B Do you remember?

Is the sentence expressing disbelief, or is it saying you don't know? Write D (disbelief) or DK (don't know). You have one minute.

1 I have no idea. ______
2 Seriously? ______
3 No way! ______
4 I don't believe it! ______
5 I don't have a clue. ______
6 I really don't know. ______

Lesson C Test your partner!

Say three comparative adjectives. Can your partner use the superlative forms in a sentence? Take turns. You have three minutes.

A: *More famous.*

B: *The most famous. The most famous person I've ever met is George Clooney.*

Lesson D Guess!

Describe a natural wonder in your country, but don't say its name. Can your partner guess what it is? You have two minutes.

2 In the real world

What are the seven wonders of the modern world? Go online or to a library, and find information in English about the seven wonders of the modern world. Choose one and write about it.

A Wonder of the Modern World

The Itaipu Dam is one of the seven wonders of the modern world. It's on the Paraná River between Brazil and Paraguay. Many people in South America depend on the dam for power and electricity. About 40,000 workers helped construct the dam, and it's one of the most expensive objects ever built. It's also huge. In fact, it's so big that . . .

6 Organizing your time

Lesson A
- Commitments
- Present tenses used for future

Lesson B
- Offering to take a message
- Leaving a message

Lesson C
- Favors
- Requests; promises and offers with *will*

Lesson D
- Reading "Time and Culture"
- Writing: Tips for success

Warm Up

A Look at the pictures. What's happening? Do you think the people in the photos organize their time well?

B Do you think you organize your time well? Why or why not?

A A busy week

1 Vocabulary Commitments

A Match the words in columns A and B. Then listen and check your answers.

	A	B
1	a birthday	appointment
2	a blind	call
3	a business	date
4	a conference	interview
5	a doctor's	lesson
6	a job	meeting
7	soccer	party
8	a violin	practice

B PAIR WORK When was the last time you had each commitment? Tell your partner.

2 Language in context Weekend plans

A Read George's plans for the weekend. Number the pictures from 1 to 8.

My parents are arriving from out of town this weekend. I'm picking them up at the airport on Friday night. Their flight doesn't get in until midnight. They're staying at my place for a couple of weeks. On Saturday, I'm preparing breakfast for them. Then I have a doctor's appointment. In the afternoon, I'm taking them for a drive around town. In the evening, I'm starting a new part-time job. There's a new movie I want to see on Sunday. I'm going with a friend of mine from school. It starts at 9:00 p.m., so we're having dinner first.

B Which things in Part A do you think George will enjoy? Do you have any of the same plans?

3 Grammar Present tenses used for future

Use the present continuous to describe plans or intentions.
My parents **are arriving** from out of town this weekend.
They**'re staying** at my place for the weekend.
Use the simple present to describe events that are on a schedule or a timetable.
I **have** an appointment in the morning.
The movie **starts** at 9:00 p.m.

A Complete the conversation with the present continuous or the simple present forms of the verbs. Then practice with a partner.

A What ________ you ________ (do) tonight?
B Oh, I ________ (take) my sister to the airport. She ________ (go) to Manila. Her flight ________ (leave) at 9:00.
A ________ you ________ (do) anything tomorrow?
B I ________ (have) soccer practice at 2:00.

B PAIR WORK What are your plans after class? Tell your partner.

4 Listening A weekend away

A Listen to Peter talk with his neighbor Nancy. Check (✓) the true sentences.

1 ☐ Nancy has a date this weekend. ________
2 ☐ Peter's train leaves Friday night at 8:30. ________
3 ☐ Peter's grandfather is turning 70. ________
4 ☐ Peter and Kevin are going to museums on Sunday. ________
5 ☐ Peter and Kevin arrive home on Sunday evening. ________
6 ☐ Peter has a job interview on Monday. ________

B Listen again. Correct the false sentences.

5 Speaking What are you doing this weekend?

A CLASS ACTIVITY Find classmates who are going to do each thing. Write their names and ask questions for more information.

Find someone who . . . this weekend.	Name	Extra information
is going out		
is planning to stay home		
has a lesson or an appointment		
plans to meet friends		
is spending time with relatives		

B Who has the most interesting plans? What are they?

6 Keep talking!

Go to page 135 for more practice.

I can ask and talk about weekend plans.

B Can I take a message?

1 Interactions Phone messages

A How many phone calls do you make in a week? Do you leave many messages?

B Listen to the conversation. What message does Rex leave for Jake? Then practice the conversation.

Ben Hello?

Rex Hi. Can I please speak to Jake?

Ben Um, sorry. Jake's not here right now. I think he might be at the gym. Can I take a message?

Rex Uh, sure. This is Rex Hanson. I'm calling about our class trip. Please tell him that we're leaving tomorrow at 8:00, not 9:00.

Ben OK, got it. I'll give him the message.

Rex Great. Thanks a lot. Bye.

Ben Good-bye.

C Read the expressions below. Complete each box with a similar expression from the conversation. Then listen and check your answers.

Offering to take a message

____

Do you want to leave a message?

Would you like to leave a message?

Leaving a message

____

Can you tell . . . that . . . ?

Could you let . . . know that . . . ?

D PAIR WORK Have conversations like the one in Part B. Use these ideas.

You're calling your friend Carrie at home, but she's at soccer practice.
She needs to bring her laptop to class.

You're calling your friend Gary at work, but he's in a meeting.
The birthday party starts at 7:00, not 8:00.

2 Listening Taking messages

A Listen to four people leave phone messages. Number the messages from 1 to 4.

☐
MANHATTAN DESIGNS
TO: MR. PHILIPS
FROM: JULIE KIM
TIME: 2:45
MESSAGE: SHE NEEDS THE ______________
FOR HER OFFICE BY ______________.

☐
Silvia—
______________ Miller's office called. You should come in for your ______________ at 4:30, not 3:00.
– Beth

☐
Paul,
Your ______________ Kurt called. Your parents' anniversary party is at his place, not your ______________.

☐
MESSAGE
To: Roberto
From: Hank
Message:
______________ is canceled
______________.

B Listen again. Complete the messages.

C Listen to the people return the calls. What happens to whom? Write M (Mr. Philips), P (Paul), R (Roberto), or S (Silvia).

1 ______ gets a busy signal.
2 ______ gets disconnected.
3 ______ leaves a voicemail.
4 ______ calls the wrong number.

3 Speaking Role play

A Complete the chart with your own ideas.

	Who's the message for?	What's the message about?	What's the message?
1	Rosario	soccer practice	She needs to come 15 minutes early.
2		the meeting	It's on Thursday, not Tuesday. It's still at 4:00.
3	Jennifer		It starts at 10:00p.m. Bring dancing shoes.
4		the job interview	
5			

B PAIR WORK Role-play the phone conversations. Then change roles.

Student A: Call the people in the chart. They can't talk, so leave messages for them.

Student B: Answer the phone. Explain why the people can't talk, and offer to take messages for them.

I can offer to take a message. ✓
I can leave a message. ✓

C Can you do me a favor?

1 Vocabulary Favors

A Match the phrases and the pictures. Then listen and check your answers.

a	check my homework	c	get my mail	e	help me with my résumé	g	pick me up
b	feed my cat	d	give me a ride	f	lend me some money	h	water my plants

1  ☐

2  ☐

3  ☐

4  ☐

5  ☐

6  ☐

7  ☐

8  ☐

B PAIR WORK **Who might you ask to do each thing in Part A? Discuss your ideas.**

a child	a classmate	a friend	a neighbor	a parent	a teacher

2 Conversation Is that all?

A Listen to the conversation. What things does Kate ask Ruth to do for her?

Ruth Oh, hi, Kate. What's up?

Kate Hi, Ruth. Listen, I'm going away this weekend. Can you do me a favor?

Ruth Sure. What do you need?

Kate Can you feed my cat, please?

Ruth No problem. I'll feed her. Is that all?

Kate Well, could you please get my mail, too?

Ruth Sure. I could do that for you. I'll put it on your kitchen table. Anything else?

Kate If you don't mind, there's one more thing.

Ruth What's that?

Kate I'm getting back at 11:00 on Sunday night. Would you mind picking me up at the airport?

B Listen to the rest of the conversation. Why can't Ruth pick Kate up?

3 Grammar Requests; promises and offers with *will*

Requests	Promises and offers
Can you **feed** my cat, please?	No problem. **I'll feed** her.
Could you please **get** my mail?	Sure. **I'll put** it on your kitchen table.
Would you **pick** me up at the airport?	All right. **I won't be** late. I promise.
Would you **mind picking** me up at the airport?	No, I don't mind. I'**ll be** there.

A Match the requests and the responses. Then practice with a partner.

1 Can you lend me your car tonight? ____
2 Ms. Smith, would you check my homework, please? ____
3 Can you give me a ride to class? ____
4 Would you mind feeding my fish? ____
5 Could you water my plants this weekend? ____
6 Would you mind picking me up at the mall? ____

a. Sure. I'll look at it after I help Michael.
b. No problem. I'll do it on Saturday.
c. Not at all. What time?
d. I guess so. I'll give you the keys after I pick up Rachel from school.
e. Yeah, sure. I'll be at your house at 10:00.
f. No, I don't mind. I'll feed them after work.

B PAIR WORK **Ask and answer the questions in Part A. Answer with your own offer or promise.**

4 Pronunciation Reduction of *could you* and *would you*

A Listen and repeat. Notice how *could you* and *would you* are sometimes pronounced /kʊdʒə/ and /wʊdʒə/.

Could you please get my mail? **Would you** pick me up at the airport?

B PAIR WORK **Practice requests with *could you*, *would you*, and the phrases from Exercise 1. Reduce *could you* and *would you*.**

5 Speaking Unfavorable favors

A Think of three favors to ask your classmates. Use the ideas below or your own ideas. Be creative!

feed my pet snake	lend me some money
check my homework	lend me your cell phone
help me clean my room	make my lunch

B CLASS ACTIVITY **Find three different classmates to do the favors for you. If you decline a request, make an excuse. If you accept a request, make an offer or a promise.**

6 Keep talking!

Go to page 136 for more practice.

I can make requests, promises, and offers.

D Perspectives on time

1 Reading

A Do you have a busy schedule? Or do you find time to relax?

B Read the article. Do you identify more with the Germans or Italians?

PERSPECTIVE ON TIME

Time and Culture

Imagine you're going to a party this weekend at your friend's apartment. "Could you come at 7 p.m. and bring dessert?" she asked. What time do you think you'll actually arrive? Ten minutes early? Half an hour late? Right on time?

The answer probably depends on your cultural view of time. Different cultures and countries have very different ways of thinking about time. Even countries that are quite close to each other like Germany and Italy see time very differently.

Deadlines and Meeting Times

There is a saying in countries like Germany and the U.S., "Time is money." People think of wasting time as the same as wasting or losing money. If you miss a deadline or are late to a meeting, people might get mad. In other countries like Italy and Greece, people are less strict about deadlines and appointments. Meetings and conversations start and end when it feels right, not when the clock strikes 2 p.m.

Getting Things Done vs. Building Relationships

In many Western countries, people want to get as much done in as little time as possible. They get impatient if decisions are not made fast enough. In other countries, taking time to build relationships is more important than getting things done fast. That's why meetings often start with lots of small talk before getting down to business.

Pace of Life

In some countries, it almost seems that people are in a race to get through life as quickly and efficiently as possible. In other countries, life is more about enjoying time—sharing meals, taking walks and spending time with friends and family.

As you travel or make friends with people from other cultures, it can help to improve communication if you understand their perspectives on time.

C Read the article again. Write three differences between the way people view time in Germany and Italy.

In Germany...	In Italy...
People want to get a lot done.	People want to enjoy life.

D PAIR WORK How do you view time in your culture? What about in your family? Does everyone in one country or culture share the same view of time?

2 Writing Tips for success

A GROUP WORK **Choose one of the topics below or your own idea. What tips for success can you think of? Discuss your ideas and make a list of your tips.**

how to find more time for family	how to remember important things
how to make and keep friends	how to study better

B GROUP WORK **Create a poster with the most useful tips. Write a short paragraph for each tip.**

C CLASS ACTIVITY **Present your tips for success. Ask and answer questions for more information.**

HOW TO DEVELOP BETTER STUDY HABITS

1 **Take regular breaks.**

It's important to take breaks. Get up and stretch, go for a walk, or call a friend for a chat. You'll feel ready for more!

2 **Listen to music.**

Listen to relaxing music. This helps you…

3 Speaking Time management interview

A PAIR WORK **Interview your partner. Check (✓) his or her answers.**

Are you overdoing things?

Do you…?	Often	Sometimes	Never
get nervous when you have to wait	☐	☐	☐
feel like you do things too quickly	☐	☐	☐
often do two or more things at once	☐	☐	☐
feel bad when you're not working or studying	☐	☐	☐
feel like things don't move fast enough for you	☐	☐	☐
forget important events, like birthdays	☐	☐	☐
get angry in situations you can't control	☐	☐	☐
get bored easily when you're not working or studying	☐	☐	☐
get angry when you make small mistakes	☐	☐	☐
make big decisions before you get all the facts	☐	☐	☐

B PAIR WORK **Score your partner's answers. Add 2 for *often*, 1 for *sometimes*, and 0 for *never*. Tell your partner the results.**

13-20 You're overdoing it.
You probably already know you're too busy. Take a deep breath and slow down.

7-12 You're overdoing it a little.
You're doing well, but try not to do too much. Make sure you make time for yourself.

0-6 You're not overdoing it.
Congratulations! You are managing your time well. Keep it up!

C PAIR WORK **Are you overdoing it? If so, what time-management tips can help? Discuss your ideas.**

I can discuss ways to manage time effectively.

Wrap-up

1 Quick pair review

Lesson A Find out!

What are two commitments both you and your partner have next month? You have two minutes.

A: *I'm going to a conference for work next month. Are you?*

B: *No, I'm not, but I have a dentist's appointment next month. Do you?*

A: . . .

Lesson B Brainstorm!

Make a list of three ways to offer to take a message and three ways to leave one. You have two minutes.

Lesson C Do you remember?

Match the requests and the responses. You have two minutes.

1 Could you water my plants for me? ______
2 Would you mind giving me a ride to work? ______
3 Can you feed my dog, please? ______
4 Could you please call me back at 4:00? ______
5 Can you meet me in the library tomorrow? ______

a. OK. I'll call your cell phone.
b. Sure. I'll water them.
c. Yes. I'll bring my books so we can study.
d. Yeah, I'll do that. What does he eat?
e. No problem. I'll pick you up at 8:00.

Lesson D Give your opinion!

What three tips can you give someone who is always late for class? Decide together. You have two minutes.

2 In the real world

What are some tips for success? Go online and find tips in English about one of these topics or your own idea. Then write about them.

how to get rich	how to make a good first impression
how to improve your pronunciation	how to write a good résumé

How to Save Money

It's important to save money every month. One way to save money is to turn off the lights when you aren't using them, because electricity is expensive. Another way to save money is to cook at home more often. Food can be very expensive, especially if you eat out a lot. You should look for discounts online. Also, . . .

7 Personalities

Lesson A
- Personality traits
- Adverbs modifying adjectives and verbs

Lesson B
- Giving an opinion
- Asking for agreement

Lesson C
- More personality traits
- Present perfect with *for* and *since*

Lesson D
- Reading "The Signs of the Zodiac"
- Writing: My personality

Warm Up

A Describe the people in the picture. Where are they? What are they doing?

B What do you think each person is like? Why?

A You're extremely curious.

1 Vocabulary Personality traits

A **Match the adjectives and the sentences. Then listen and check your answers.**

1 adventurous ____
2 ambitious ____
3 careful ____
4 curious ____
5 easygoing ____
6 optimistic ____
7 outgoing ____
8 stubborn ____

a. I'm interested in learning about people and things around me.
b. I'm friendly, and I like people.
c. I set high goals for myself.
d. I look on the bright side of things.
e. I do things slowly and with attention to detail.
f. I don't like to change my mind.
g. I am relaxed, and I don't worry about little things.
h. I love trying new, exciting activities.

B **PAIR WORK** **Describe people you know with each personality trait. Tell your partner.**

"My baby brother is very curious about the world. He wants to touch everything."

2 Language in context Are you a believer?

A **Read the personality descriptions. Underline the positive personality traits, and circle the negative ones.**

Are You Adventurous?

Answer ten questions in this quick personality test to find out just how adventurous you are!

Click here to begin.

Year of the Monkey

Born in years 1968, 1980, 1992, and 2004

You're extremely curious and outgoing. You solve problems well, but you can be stubborn about some things.

Personality Test Results

Your score: 13

You're very adventurous, but you're not a very careful person. Try not to make decisions quickly. Take time to consider your options seriously.

Your Birth Order

As the first-born child in your family, you are a natural leader. You're pretty ambitious and like to work hard. However, you don't work well without direction.

B **What about you? Do you believe the things in Part A can tell you about your personality? Why or why not?**

3 Grammar Adverbs modifying adjectives and verbs

Adverbs that modify adjectives come before the adjectives.

You're **pretty** ambitious.

You're **extremely** curious and outgoing.

Adverbs that modify verbs go after the verb or the verb and its object.

You don't work **well** without direction.

Try not to make decisions **quickly**.

Turn to page 152 for a list of adjective and adverb formations.

A Add the adverbs to the sentences. Then compare with a partner.

1. I move slowly in the morning. (slowly)
2. I'm serious about my studies. (really)
3. I choose my words. (carefully)
4. I arrive at important meetings. (early)
5. My friends are important to me. (extremely)
6. I work in large groups. (well)
7. I'm optimistic about the future. (very)
8. It's easy for me to share my feelings. (fairly)

B PAIR WORK Which sentences in Part A are true for you? Tell your partner.

4 Speaking My true self

A PAIR WORK Interview your partner and ask questions for more information. Take notes.

	Name: ______	Yes	No	Extra information
1	Are you very adventurous?	☐	☐	
2	Do you make new friends easily?	☐	☐	
3	Do you make decisions quickly?	☐	☐	
4	Are you really stubborn about anything?	☐	☐	
5	Do you work and study hard?	☐	☐	
6	Do you get to class early?	☐	☐	
7	Are you completely honest all the time?	☐	☐	

A: Are you very adventurous?
B: Yes, I think so.
A: What's the most adventurous thing you've ever done?

B PAIR WORK Share the most interesting information with another partner.

5 Keep talking!

Go to page 137 for more practice.

I can talk about personality traits.

B In my opinion, . . .

1 Interactions Opinions

A **Do you always tell people exactly what you think? Do you sometimes keep your opinions to yourself?**

B **Listen to the conversation. Whose opinion do you agree with more? Then practice the conversation.**

Fei Have you seen Adam's new painting?

Ralph Yes. I saw it last weekend.

Fei It's not very good.

Ralph No, it's not. He asked me what I thought of it. I said I didn't think it was his best painting.

Fei You're kidding! How did he react?

Ralph He didn't seem very happy to hear that. But he did ask.

Fei In my opinion, it's better to say something positive, even if you don't really mean it. Don't you agree?

Ralph I don't know. Why do you say that?

Fei Well, it's not always easy to hear the truth.

Ralph I'm not so sure. I find that honesty is always the best policy.

C **Read the expressions below. Complete each box with a similar expression from the conversation. Then listen and check your answers.**

Giving an opinion	Asking for agreement
______________	______________
If you ask me, . . .	Don't you think so?
Maybe it's just me, but I think . . .	Don't you think that's true?

D PAIR WORK **Check (✓) the opinions you agree with. Then ask your partner for agreement.**

1 ☐ Women are more stubborn than men.
☐ Men are more stubborn than women.

2 ☐ It's never OK to lie.
☐ It's sometimes OK to lie.

3 ☐ A small group of friends is better than a large group of friends.
☐ A large group of friends is better than a small group of friends.

2 Pronunciation Reduction of *don't you*

A 🎧 **Listen and repeat. Notice how *don't you* is pronounced /downtʃə/.**

Don't you agree? Don't you think so? Don't you think that's true?

B PAIR WORK **Say the opinions in Exercise 1D again. Ask your partner for agreement. Reduce *don't you* to /downtʃə/.**

3 Listening A book of proverbs

A 🎧 **Listen to Tina and Cal talk about proverbs. Number the proverbs from 1 to 4 in the order you hear them.**

Proverbs	Does Tina agree?	Does Cal agree?
☐ Practice makes perfect.	yes / no	yes / no
☐ Better late than never.	yes / no	yes / no
☐ Beauty is only skin deep.	yes / no	yes / no
☐ Two heads are better than one.	yes / no	yes / no

B 🎧 **Listen again. Do Tina and Cal agree with the proverbs in Part A? Circle *yes* or *no*.**

C PAIR WORK **Do you agree with each proverb? Why or why not? Do you know any similar proverbs in your own language? Tell your partner.**

4 Speaking Don't you think so?

A **What's your opinion? Circle the words.**

1. People are **more** / **less** ambitious these days.
2. Young people are **more** / **less** optimistic than older people.
3. **First-born** / **Last-born** children are usually very easygoing.
4. It's **possible** / **impossible** to change your personality.

B GROUP WORK **Discuss your opinions from Part A.**

A: If you ask me, people are less ambitious these days. Don't you think so?
B: I'm not so sure. Why do you say that?
C: Well, maybe it's just me, but I feel no one wants to work hard these days.
D: I'm not sure I really agree. In my opinion, . . .

C GROUP WORK **Think of three other topics. Share your opinions about them. Does anyone agree with you?**

"In my opinion, people worry about their appearance too much. Don't you agree?"

I can give an opinion. ✓
I can ask for agreement. ✓

C We've been friends for six years.

1 Vocabulary More personality traits

A Match the adjectives and the definitions. Then listen and check your answers.

1 agreeable ______	a. thinking of the needs of others
2 considerate ______	b. treating people equally or right
3 decisive ______	c. friendly and pleasing
4 fair ______	d. making decisions quickly

5 honest ______	e. waiting without getting annoyed
6 mature ______	f. doing what is expected or promised
7 patient ______	g. truthful
8 reliable ______	h. behaving in a responsible way

B Complete the chart with the opposites of the words in Part A. Then listen and check your answers.

dis-	im-	in-	un-
disagreeable			

C PAIR WORK What are the three best personality traits to have in a friend? What are the three worst? Discuss your ideas.

2 Conversation Time to say you're sorry

A Listen to the conversation. How does Lance describe Jill's reaction?

Lance I don't know what to do about my friend Jill. I haven't spoken to her since last weekend, and she won't answer my text messages.

Emily Did something happen?

Lance Yeah. I said something about her to another friend. She found out, and now I feel terrible. To be honest, it wasn't anything serious, though. I think she's being unfair and a little immature.

Emily Well, put yourself in her shoes. Imagine a friend saying something about you behind your back.

Lance You're probably right.

Emily Have you been friends for a long time?

Lance Yes. We've been friends for six years, and we used to talk all the time.

Emily Then I think you should do the considerate thing and call to say you're sorry.

B Listen to Lance and Jill's phone conversation. What word does Lance use to describe himself?

3 Grammar Present perfect with *for* and *since*

Use the present perfect to describe an action that began in the past and continues to now. Use for *to specify the amount of time. Use* since *to specify the starting point.*

How long have you been friends?
We've been friends **for six years.**
We've been friends **since middle school.**

She's been upset **for several days.**

I haven't spoken to her **since last weekend.**

for	since
ten minutes	3:00
two hours	last night
several days	Monday
a month	October
six years	2009
a long time	high school
quite a while	I was a kid

A Complete the sentences with *for* or *since*. Then compare with a partner.

1 Rod has become more considerate ______ he got married.
2 Mr. and Mrs. Kim haven't had an argument ______ 1981.
3 Pete and Lisa have been on the phone ______ six hours.
4 Tim hasn't spoken with his brother ______ a long time.
5 Jay's been totally unreliable ______ he started his new job.
6 Inez has been in her new job ______ three months.
7 Annie has become less immature ______ high school.
8 Jessica and Hector have been married ______ 25 years.

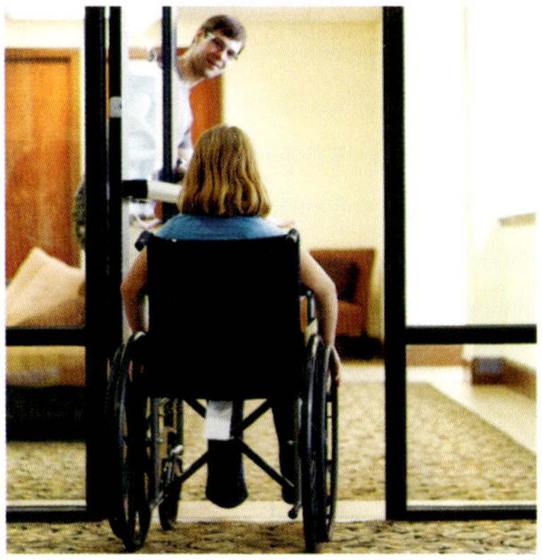

B PAIR WORK Ask and answer the questions.

1 How long have you been in this class?
2 What haven't you done since you were a kid?
3 What have you wanted to do for a long time?

4 Speaking Three friends

A Think of three friends. Complete the chart.

	Names	How long we've been friends	Their personality traits
1			
2			
3			

B GROUP WORK Tell your group about your friends. Use your information from Part A. Ask and answer questions for more information.

A: I've known my friend Jesse since middle school.
B: What's he like?
A: He's very honest and reliable.

5 Keep talking!

Go to page 138 for more practice.

I can describe people's personalities.

D What is your personality?

1 Reading

A When were you born? Read the description of your zodiac sign. Does it describe you well?

4:21PM

THE SIGNS OF THE ZODIAC

Capricorn Dec. 22 – Jan. 20
You're ambitious and good at business, but you sometimes worry about things too much.

Aquarius Jan. 21 – Feb. 19
You're creative and care about other people's feelings, but you can sometimes be difficult to work with.

Pisces Feb. 20 – March 20
You're considerate, but sometimes you don't help yourself enough. You decide things quickly and rarely change your mind.

Aries March 21 – April 20
You're optimistic and creative. You know what you want, but you sometimes have difficulty sharing your feelings.

Taurus April 21 – May 21
You're talkative and always say exactly what you think. You work hard, but you can get angry quickly.

Gemini May 22 – June 21
You like adventure. You love to try new things and can be very creative. You can sometimes be unreliable.

Cancer June 22 – July 22
You're very patient and want everyone to get along, but you can have difficulty showing your feelings.

Leo July 23 – Aug. 23
You're a leader. You like to give, but you don't like to ask for things. You're not very patient.

Virgo Aug. 24 – Sept. 22
You're ambitious and want things done with no mistakes. You are not always open to new ideas.

Libra Sept. 23 – Oct. 22
You get along with everyone and are curious about many things. You're always looking for something better.

Scorpio Oct. 23 – Nov. 21
You're a reliable friend, but you can have difficulty sharing your feelings. You know exactly what you want.

Sagittarius Nov. 22 – Dec. 21
You're honest – sometimes too honest. You don't always learn from your mistakes.

B Read the chart. Complete the sentences with the correct zodiac signs.

1 A/An ______________ hates asking for things.
2 A/An ______________ talks a lot.
3 A/An ______________ is good at business.
4 A/An ______________ wants everything perfect.
5 A/An ______________ is adventurous.
6 A/An ______________ is decisive.
7 A/An ______________ always tells the truth.
8 A/An ______________ is difficult to work with.

C GROUP WORK Think of three people you know. What is each person's zodiac sign? Does it describe their personalities well? Tell your group.

2 Listening Imagine you're in a forest . . .

A Listen to the personality test. Number the questions from 1 to 7 in the order you hear them.

- ☐ What's it made of? ____________
- ☐ Who are you with? ____________
- ☐ What do you do with it? ____________
- ☐ How big is it? ____________
- ☐ What kind do you see? ____________
- ☐ What's on the table? ____________
- ☐ Is it open or closed? ____________

B Listen again. Now take the personality test. Answer the questions with your own ideas.

C PAIR WORK Compare your answers. Then turn to page 153 to see what your answers mean.

3 Writing and speaking My personality

A Think about your personality. Answer the questions.

- What are your positive personality traits? ____________
- Are there any traits you'd like to change? ____________
- Has your personality changed through the years? If so, how? ____________

____

B Write a paragraph about your personality, but do not write your name! Use the model and your answers in Part A to help you.

What am I like?

I'm a pretty easygoing and outgoing person. I'm also very optimistic about the future. I think people like to be around me. However, I can be stubborn sometimes . . .

C GROUP WORK Put your papers facedown on the table. Take one paper and read the description. Your group guesses who it is and agrees or disagrees with the description. Take turns.

A: *I think that paragraph describes Dana.*

B: *Yes, that's right. I wrote that one.*

C: *I agree you're easygoing, Dana, but I don't really think you're stubborn.*

B: *Yes, I am!*

I can talk about my personality. ✓

Wrap-up

1 Quick pair review

Lesson A Test your partner!

Say an adjective. Can your partner write the adverb form correctly? Take turns. You have two minutes.

"Careful."

1 carefully ______ 3 ______ 5 ______

2 ______ 4 ______ 6 ______

Lesson B Give your opinion!

Look at the two pieces of art. What do you think of them? Give two opinions about each one. You have two minutes.

A: If you ask me, I think the sculpture is weird. Don't you think so?

B: In my opinion, it's very interesting.

Lesson C Brainstorm!

Make a list of positive and negative personality traits. How many do you know? You have two minutes.

Lesson D Find out!

Who are two people that you and your partner know with the same personality traits. You have two minutes.

A: My friend John is really stubborn. Do you know a stubborn person?

B: Yes. My little sister!

2 In the real world

What's your zodiac sign? Find your horoscope from yesterday or last week in an English-language newspaper, magazine, or website. Was it true? Write about it.

My Horoscope

I'm a Pisces. My horoscope last week said, "You are going to have a difficult day at work." It was true. I was very busy and nervous because I had to give a presentation. Luckily, it went very well!

8 The environment

Lesson A
- Environmental impacts
- Quantifiers

Lesson B
- Giving an approximate answer
- Avoiding answering

Lesson C
- Tips to help the environment
- First conditional

Lesson D
- Reading "One-of-a-Kind Homes"
- Writing: Local concerns

Warm Up

A Look at the "before" and "after" pictures. What do you see? What has changed?

B Which was the biggest improvement? Which was the easiest to do? Which was the most difficult?

A Going green

1 Vocabulary Environmental impacts

A Label the pictures with the correct words. Then listen and check your answers.

e-waste	hybrid car	organic food	pollution	solar energy
global warming	nuclear energy	plastic bags	recycling bin	wind farm

1 ______________

2 ______________

3 ______________

4 ______________

5 ______________

6 ______________

7 ______________

8 ______________

9 ______________

10 ______________

B PAIR WORK How do the things in Part A impact the environment?

2 Language in context Green products

A Read the ads. What makes each product "green"?

B What about you? Do you own any green products? Would you buy these?

3 Grammar Quantifiers

Quantifiers with count nouns	Quantifiers with noncount nouns
We need **more** wind farms.	You can save **more** money with CFLs.
There are**n't enough** recycling bins.	People do**n't** buy **enough** organic food.
There are **too many** bottles in landfills.	Regular lightbulbs use **too much** energy.
People should buy **fewer** plastic bottles.	People should try to use **less** plastic.

A Complete the opinions with quantifiers. Then compare with a partner.

1 "I think it's good that ________ people are buying hybrid cars. They reduce global warming."
2 "In my opinion there's ________ e-waste in our landfills. We need better and safer ways to recycle electronics."
3 "Farmers should grow ________ organic food. I prefer food without chemicals."
4 "Unfortunately, not ________ people use solar power. Is it because it's expensive?"
5 "I feel people should use ________ nuclear energy. Isn't it dangerous?"
6 "Some people say they don't have ________ time to recycle. That's crazy!"
7 "Maybe it's just me, but I think shoppers should take ________ plastic and paper bags from the supermarket. I always bring my own bags."
8 "________ people throw plastic bottles in garbage cans. They should use recycling bins."

B PAIR WORK Do you agree with the opinions in Part A? Why or why not? Tell your partner.

4 Pronunciation Stress in compound nouns

A Listen and repeat. Notice how the first noun in compound nouns often receives stronger stress.

landfill **light**bulb **travel** case **water** bottle

B PAIR WORK Practice the compound nouns. Stress the first noun.

toothbrush garbage can recycling bin wind farm

5 Speaking Our community

A PAIR WORK What environmental problems does your community have? Complete the sentences.

1 There's too much ________.
2 There isn't enough ________.
3 We should have fewer ________.
4 There are too many ________.
5 There aren't enough ________.
6 We should use less ________.

B GROUP WORK Share your ideas with another pair. Did you identify the same problems? Which are the most important?

6 Keep talking!

Go to page 139 for more practice.

I can discuss environmental problems.

B I'd rather not say.

1 Interactions Answering and avoiding answering

A **Imagine these people are asking you questions. Are there any questions they might ask that you think are too personal and that you would not answer?**

a doctor	a friend	a neighbor	a parent	a stranger	a teacher

B **Listen to the conversation. What question doesn't Jim answer? Then practice the conversation.**

Carl So, Jim, how's the new car?

Jim Hey, Carl. It's great. I'm really happy with it.

Carl It's a hybrid, isn't it?

Jim Yeah. It causes less pollution. I'm trying to do my part to help the environment, you know?

Carl That's great. How long have you had it?

Jim I've only had it for a week.

Carl Really? How many kilometers have you driven?

Jim I'd say about 150.

Carl So, how does it run?

Jim Oh, it runs very well. I'll give you a ride later if you want.

Carl OK, thanks. How much did it cost exactly?

Jim Actually, I'd rather not say. But I know I made a good purchase.

C **Read the expressions below. Complete each box with a similar expression from the conversation. Then listen and check your answers.**

Giving an approximate answer

____

I'd say maybe . . .

Probably . . .

Avoiding answering

____

I'd prefer not to say.

I'd rather not answer that.

D **Match the questions and the responses. Then practice with a partner.**

1 How often do you drive? ______

2 How much do you drive every day? ______

3 How many people have you given rides to? ______

4 How much did you sell your old car for? ______

a. I'd say about ten.

b. Probably five or six times a week.

c. I'd rather not answer that.

d. I'd say about 30 minutes.

2 Listening Consumer research

A 🎧 **Listen to a man answer survey questions in a grocery store. Number the questions from 1 to 9 in the order you hear them.**

- ☐ Have your buying habits changed in the last year? ______
- ☐1 How often do you walk to the grocery store? All the time.
- ☐ Do you usually ask for paper or plastic bags? ______
- ☐ How much do you spend on groceries every month? ______
- ☐ How many people are there in your household? ______
- ☐ What is the highest level of education you've completed? ______
- ☐ What do you do for a living? ______
- ☐ Do you ever shop for groceries online? ______
- ☐ How often do you buy environmentally friendly products? ______

B 🎧 **Listen again. Write the man's answers.**

C PAIR WORK **Ask and answer the questions in Part A. Answer with your own information, or avoid answering.**

3 Speaking Do you waste water?

A **Read the survey. Are there any questions you would avoid answering, or is there any information you wouldn't share?**

WATER USE SURVEY

Name: ______ Phone number: ______

Address: ______ Email: ______

Age: ______ Education: ______

How many showers do you take in a week? ______

How long do you spend in the shower? ______

Do you ever leave the water running when you brush your teeth? ______

Do you wash dishes by hand or do you use a dishwasher? ______

When you wash dishes, do you leave the water running? ______

When you wash clothes, is the washing machine always completely full? ______

Do you flush the toilet after every use? ______

B PAIR WORK **Interview your partner. Complete the survey with his or her answers. Mark an ✗ if he or she avoids answering.**

C PAIR WORK **Compare your answers. Who uses more water? How could you use less water?**

I can give an approximate answer. ✓

I can avoid answering. ✓

C What will happen?

1 Vocabulary Tips to help the environment

A Match the tips and the pictures. Then listen and check your answers.

a	Buy local food.	d	Pay bills online.	g	Use cloth shopping bags.
b	Fix leaky faucets.	e	Take public transportation.	h	Use rechargeable batteries.
c	Grow your own food.	f	Use a clothesline.		

1 ☐ 

2 ☐ 

3 ☐ 

4 ☐ 

5 ☐ 

6 ☐ 

7 ☐ 

8 ☐ 

B PAIR WORK **Which things in Part A do you do now? Which don't you do? Tell your partner.**

2 Conversation This is awful!

A **Listen to the conversation. When does Kendra want to start taking public transportation?**

Ina This is awful! It's taking forever to get to work.

Kendra I know. There are just too many cars these days! The traffic seems to get worse and worse.

Ina Maybe we should start taking public transportation. If we take the subway, we won't have to sit in traffic.

Kendra And we might save money if we take the subway.

Ina I think you're right. Also, if we take public transportation, we won't get stressed out before work. So, when do we start?

Kendra How about tomorrow?

B **Listen to their conversation the next day. What are they unhappy about?**

3 Grammar First conditional

First conditional sentences describe real possibilities. Use the present tense in the if *clause (the condition). Use* will *in the main clause.*

If we **take** public transportation, we**'ll save** money.
If we **take** public transportation, we **won't get** stressed out.
Air pollution **will get** worse if we **don't reduce** the number of cars.

Use modals such as may, might, *or* could *in the main clause when you're less certain about the results.*

If air pollution **gets** worse, more people **may get** sick.
If you **don't fix** your leaky faucet, you **might get** a high water bill.
You **could spend** money on other things if you **grow** your own food.

A Write first conditional sentences with the two clauses. Then compare with a partner.

1 you'll use 60 percent less energy / you replace your regular lightbulbs with CFLs
You'll use 60 percent less energy if you replace your regular lightbulbs with CFLs.

2 you pay your bills online / you'll use less paper
____________________________.

3 we fix our leaky faucets / we'll save water
____________________________.

4 there won't be much air pollution / everyone uses hybrid cars
____________________________.

5 you use a clothesline / other people may start to do the same
____________________________.

6 we use rechargeable batteries / we could save a lot of money
____________________________.

B PAIR WORK What else will or may happen for each condition in Part A? Discuss your ideas.

A: *What else will happen if you replace your regular lightbulbs with CFLs?*
B: *If I replace my regular lightbulbs with CFLs, I'll have cheaper electric bills.*

4 Speaking Around the circle

A Write a sentence about what will happen if you change a habit to become greener.

If I grow my own food, I will eat better.

B GROUP WORK Sit in a circle. Go around the circle and share your ideas. Repeat your classmates' main clauses as conditions, and add new ideas.

A: *If I grow my own food, I will eat better.*
B: *If you eat better, you will feel healthier.*
C: *If you feel healthier, you won't need to go to the doctor very often.*

5 Keep talking!

Go to page 140 for more practice.

I can talk about future possibilities.

D Finding solutions

1 Reading

A Look at the pictures. Which home would you prefer to live in? Why?

B Read the article. Write the captions under the correct pictures.

The Recycled-Tire House	The Found-Object House	The Greenhouse

One-of-a-Kind Homes

____

Shoichi wanted to live in an environmentally friendly home, and he always liked the greenhouses in his neighborhood in Tokyo, Japan. So he decided to create his own greenhouse-style home. Sunlight warms his new home, and a plastic cover around the house helps to keep the heat inside. There aren't any walls or rooms. The "rooms" are actually large boxes on wheels. He can move them anywhere he likes, even outside. He loves his home, but sometimes he would like to be able to move the whole house.

____

Ruth is an artist who lives in the Rocky Mountains in the U.S. state of Colorado. Over the years, she found and collected a lot of old objects for her art. When she decided she wanted to live in a more unusual home, she had a creative idea. She would use many of the old materials that she collected in the home's design. For example, she used old car parts in the front door and tire rubber as the roof. She also used the door of an old car as part of a wall, so she can still lower the window!

____

Wayne and Cate are a couple from the U.S. state of Montana. They wanted a new home that wasn't too expensive. Their solution was simple – they built their own home. They recycled and used 250 old tires as the base of the house and old glass for the windows. They even used 13,000 empty soda cans in the house. Their home also has large windows and lots of plants and flowers. Solar energy keeps the house warm, even on cold days.

C Read the article again. Answer the questions.

1 What warms the inside of Shoichi's home? ______________________

2 What would Shoichi like to be able to do? ______________________

3 What creative idea did Ruth have? ______________________

4 Where are there car parts in Ruth's home? ______________________

5 Why did Wayne and Cate build their own home? ______________________

6 What did Wayne and Cate use to build their home? ______________________

D PAIR WORK **Have you heard of or seen any unique homes or buildings? Were they environmentally friendly? Tell your partner.**

2 Listening Award winners

A Listen to the conversations about two award winners, Gabriela McCall and Tayler McGillis. Who do the phrases below describe? Write T (Tayler) or G (Gabriela).

1 __T__ raised money for local charities.
2 ______ is a student in Puerto Rico.
3 ______ won an award at age 12.
4 ______ collects and recycles cans.
5 ______ helps birds.
6 ______ teaches children.
7 ______ speaks at schools about recycling.
8 ______ took photos to start a project.

B Listen again. Correct the false sentences.

1 Tayler raised more than ~~$900~~ for local charities. $9,000
2 Tayler's new goal is to collect 175,000 bottles every year. ______
3 Gabriela's project helps protect the ocean for birds in Puerto Rico. ______
4 Gabriela teaches children about recycling so that they respect the environment. ______

3 Writing and speaking Local concerns

A Write a letter to a local official about an environmental problem in your community. Use the questions and the model to help you.

- What is the problem?
- Who or what does the problem affect?
- Who or what is causing it?
- What's a solution to the problem?

Dear City Councilman,

I am a student. I am writing to tell you about the amount of noise near our school. There is a lot of construction work and traffic near our school. It is very difficult for us to study and learn during the day.

I have an idea for a possible solution to this problem. If . . .

B GROUP WORK Share your letters. Do you think the solutions will solve the problems? Can you offer other solutions?

C CLASS ACTIVITY What are the most important concerns in your community? Who else can you write to or talk to about your concerns?

I can discuss solutions to problems.

Wrap-up

1 Quick pair review

Lesson A Brainstorm!

Make a list of environmentally friendly products. How many do you know? You have two minutes.

Lesson B Do you remember?

Is the sentence giving an approximate answer, or is it avoiding answering? Write AP (approximate answer) or AV (avoiding answering). You have one minute.

How much did your car cost?

I'd say about $3,000. ______

I'd prefer not to say. ______

I'd say maybe $6,000. ______

How much trash do you throw away a week?

I'd rather not answer that. ______

I'd rather not say. ______

Probably about five bags. ______

Lesson C Give your opinion!

What do you think? Complete the sentences together. You have three minutes.

1 Our city will get cleaner if ______

2 If our school uses solar energy, ______

3 If we eat organic food, ______

4 We could recycle more if ______

Lesson D Find out!

Who is one person you know who does each thing? You have two minutes.

- Who uses environmentally friendly products at home?
- Who take public transportation to school?
- Who has taught you about an environmental issue?

A: *My aunt has solar panels on the roof of her house.*

B: *My father uses compact fluorescent lightbulbs.*

2 In the real world

How can we solve this? Go online and find information in English that gives solutions to one of these problems. Then write about them.

pollution from cars	pollution from factories
global warming	too much garbage

On Pollution Problem

If more people have hybrid cars, there will be less pollution. People can also carpool. If we share rides, there will be fewer cars on the road. Also, if we . . .

9 Relationships

Lesson A
- Relationship behaviors
- Expressions with infinitives

Lesson B
- Apologizing
- Accepting an apology

Lesson C
- Inseparable phrasal verbs
- Modals for speculating

Lesson D
- Reading "Addy's Advice"
- Writing: A piece of advice

Warm Up

A What is the relationship between the people? Number the pictures.

1 brother and sister 2 neighbors 3 co-workers 4 friends

B What do you think is happening in each picture? Do they all have good relationships?

A Healthy relationships

1 Vocabulary Relationship behaviors

A Match the words and the sentences. Then listen and check your answers.

1 apologize ______ a. No! I'm not listening to you.
2 argue ______ b. I think we really need to talk about it.
3 communicate ______ c. I'm really sorry. I didn't mean to hurt your feelings.

4 compromise ______ d. I know you're sorry. It's OK.
5 criticize ______ e. Why don't I wash the dishes and you do the laundry?
6 forgive ______ f. You're being unfair. It's your turn to take out the garbage.

7 gossip ______ g. I told her I liked her new dress, but I didn't.
8 judge ______ h. Others may disagree, but I think what you said was awful.
9 lie ______ i. Did you hear about Wendy? You'll never guess what I heard.

B PAIR WORK **Which actions from Part A should people do to have healthy relationships? Which shouldn't they do? Discuss your ideas.**

2 Language in context Relationship tips

A Read the relationship tips. Why is it a bad idea to criticize someone in front of others?

4:21PM

5 Tips for happy and healthy relationships

1. It's important to talk. It's good to communicate openly and listen carefully to others.
2. It's not a good idea to criticize someone in front of others. This can embarrass the person.
3. It's helpful to compromise in any relationship. It's not good to argue about little things.
4. It's good to forgive someone who apologizes. It's not easy to say you're sorry.
5. If you have a problem in a relationship, it's helpful to discuss it. Don't keep things inside.

B What about you? Do you agree with all the tips? Why or why not?

3 Grammar Expressions with infinitives

Use infinitives after It's + *an adjective.*

It's good **to forgive** someone.
It's important **to talk**.
It's not good **to argue**.
It's never helpful **to judge** someone.

You can also use infinitives after It's + *a noun phrase.*

It's a good idea **to accept** an apology.
It's not a good idea **to criticize** someone.

A Circle the infinitives for the best relationship advice. Then compare with a partner.

1 It's important **to lie** / **to communicate** in a relationship.
2 It's helpful **to share** / **to forget** your feelings when you have a problem.
3 It's nice **to gossip** / **to think** about other people before making decisions.
4 It's a good idea **to judge** / **to meet** new people.
5 It's useful **to discuss** / **to accept** problems.
6 It's not a good idea **to argue** / **to compromise** with your friends a lot.

B PAIR WORK Complete the sentences with your own ideas. Use *It's* expressions. Then discuss them.

1 ______________ to be a reliable friend.
2 ______________ to be honest with your parents.
3 ______________ to apologize to someone but not really mean it.
4 ______________ to say something if a friend is gossiping about you.

4 Pronunciation Sentence stress

A Listen and repeat. Notice the stress on the important words in the sentences.

It's **important** to **talk**.
It's **not good** to **argue** about **little things**.

B Listen to the sentences. Underline the stressed words.

It's helpful to compromise.
It's not easy to say you're sorry.

5 Speaking Good advice?

A PAIR WORK Choose a relationship from the list below. Then make a list of the five most important tips to make the relationship happy and healthy. Discuss your ideas.

best friends	classmates
a brother and sister	a married couple
a child and parent	a teacher and student

B GROUP WORK Share your tips with another pair. What's the best piece of advice you heard?

6 Keep talking!

Go to page 141 for more practice.

I can discuss what's important in relationships.

B I'm really sorry.

1 Interactions Apologizing

A Is it difficult for you to say you're sorry? Can you remember the last thing you apologized for?

B Listen to the conversation. What excuse does Susan give Gina? Then practice the conversation.

Gina Hello?

Susan Gina?

Gina Yeah.

Susan Hi. It's Susan.

Gina Hi, Susan.

Susan Listen, I know I missed your party last night. I'm sorry.

Gina Oh, that's OK. Is everything OK?

Susan Yeah, but you'll never believe what happened. It's kind of embarrassing. I mixed up the date.

Gina What do you mean?

Susan I thought the party was on the 31st, not the 30th.

Gina Oh, I see.

Susan So, how was the party?

Gina It was great. But we missed you!

C Read the expressions below. Complete each box with a similar expression from the conversation. Then listen and check your answers.

Apologizing	Accepting an apology
______________	______________
I'm really sorry.	Don't worry about it.
My apologies.	There's no need to apologize.

D Number the sentences from 1 to 7. Then practice with a partner.

_____ A I'm really sorry I didn't meet you at the café yesterday.

_____ A Hi. It's Greg.

_____ A Well, the repairs will be very expensive.

_____ A My car broke down, and I forgot my phone.

_____ B Is your car OK?

_____ B Don't worry about it.

_____ B Oh. Hi, Greg.

2 Listening What happened?

A Listen to four people apologize over the phone. Where did they *not* go? Number the pictures from 1 to 4.

B Listen again. Complete the excuses with the correct information.

1 I was at the ______ and completely forgot the ______ .
2 I washed my ______ last night, and the ______ was in my pocket.
3 I was out of ______ . My grandmother was in the ______ .
4 I'm in a ______ at work. I can't ______ right now.

C PAIR WORK Are all the excuses good ones? Would you accept each person's apology? Discuss your ideas.

3 Speaking Explain yourself!

A Read the situations. Write an excuse for each one. Be creative!

Situations	Excuses
You are 30 minutes late for your own wedding.	
You missed your dentist appointment.	
You didn't bring your résumé to a job interview.	
You forgot to pick up your friend.	
You didn't do your English homework.	
You broke your classmate's cell phone.	

B PAIR WORK Role-play the situations. Then change roles.

Student A: Apologize to Student B for each situation in Part A. Then make an excuse.

Student B: Ask Student A to explain each situation. Then accept the apology.

I can apologize and give excuses.

I can accept an apology.

C That can't be the problem.

1 Vocabulary Inseparable phrasal verbs

A Match the sentences. Then listen and check your answers.

1 It's awful when people **break up**. ______	a. They should call before they visit.
2 I need friends that I can **count on**. ______	b. It's always better to stay together.
3 It's not nice when friends just **drop by**. ______	c. My best friends are all reliable.

4 My family and I **get along** well. ______	d. They can be so immature.
5 My friends and I love to **get together**. ______	e. We meet every Saturday.
6 Most teenagers need to **grow up**. ______	f. We hardly ever argue.

7 People used to **pick on** me in class. ______	g. I sometimes see them at the coffee shop.
8 I love to **run into** old friends. ______	h. I'm just like her.
9 I **take after** my mother. ______	i. They were mean to me.

B PAIR WORK **Which sentences do you agree with or are true for you? Tell your partner.**

A: *I agree that it's awful when people break up, but I disagree that it's always better to stay together.*

B: *I agree with you. Some people shouldn't stay together when they argue a lot.*

2 Conversation He must be really busy.

A Listen to the conversation. What is Evan probably doing right now?

Ryan My friend Evan never seems to have time for me these days. I just can't count on him anymore.

Katie Well, he started a new job, right? He must be really busy.

Ryan Yeah, I'm sure he is. But he used to drop by or call me all the time.

Katie He might be feeling stressed out from the job. Or he could be upset with you about something.

Ryan No, that can't be the problem. I haven't done anything wrong. I think I'd better call him.

Katie Yeah, I think you should.

Ryan OK. . . . Well, there's no answer.

Katie He must still be sleeping. It's only 6:30!

B Listen to Ryan call Evan later in the day. What was the real problem with Evan?

3 Grammar Modals for speculating

Speculating with more certainty	Speculating with less certainty
He **must be** really busy. He started a new job.	He **could be** upset about something. Maybe you did something to him.
He **must not leave** his house very often. He always seems to be busy.	He **may not like** his new job. I haven't heard how he likes it.
He **can't be** upset with me. I haven't done anything to him.	He **might be feeling** stressed out. His new job may be a lot of work.

A Circle the correct words. Then compare with a partner.

1 I don't know his weekend plans. He **must** / **could** drop by on Saturday.
2 She didn't say much on the phone to him. They **must not** / **might** be getting along.
3 They **must** / **may not** come to the party. They're going out to dinner that night.
4 She **can't** / **could** take after her father. She's really tall, but he's pretty short.
5 You're coughing and sneezing so much. You **must** / **must not** be getting sick.
6 They **can't** / **might** be tired. Maybe they stayed up late to study for the test.

B Read the situations. Complete the sentences with your own ideas. Then compare with a partner.

1 Pamela and Miguel don't get along anymore. She doesn't want to talk about it.
Pamela must ______________________________.
2 Jeff just ran into his college friend Mary. He hasn't seen her for 20 years.
Jeff could ______________________________.
3 Luis and Teresa arranged to get together at a restaurant, but she never came.
Teresa may not ______________________________.
4 Brian dropped by and asked to copy your homework. You're not going to give it to him.
Brian might ______________________________.

4 Speaking Look around!

A PAIR WORK **Look around the classroom. Speculate about your classmates.**

A: I think Tom must be playing tennis later. He has his tennis racket with him today.
B: And Carmen might be happy about something. She's smiling a lot.

B CLASS ACTIVITY **Were your speculations correct? Ask your classmates.**

A: Tom, I see you have your tennis racket. Are you playing tennis later?
B: Actually, no. I played before class.

5 Keep talking!

Go to pages 142-143 for more practice.

I can speculate about people.

D Getting advice

1 Reading

A Do you ever ask for advice on the radio, TV or through social media? What kind of problems do people usually ask for help with? Do you think they are good places to ask for advice?

B Read the first few sentences of each email sent to the radio show *Addy's Advice*. Who does each person have a problem with?

Addy's Advice

1. I have a big problem. It's my best friend. She doesn't really have any time for me these days. I call her, and she can't talk. I text her, and she doesn't answer right away. I think it's because of her cat, Peaches. She got this little cat for her 30th birthday, and now she takes it everywhere. She even dresses it in little sweaters and hats. I don't know what to do. Is it possible to be jealous of a cat? **– T.J.**

2. There's this new person at work. She works next to me and we get along, but she's always asking me to do things for her. For example, she asks me to get her coffee when I get some for myself. Or she drops by and asks me to copy things for her when she's "busy." She's not my boss! Should I just refuse to do things for her? I want to be nice, but I have to do my own work. Can you help me, please? **– Marcy**

3. My little brother is driving me crazy. I'm 15, and he's 10. He has his own friends, but he won't leave me and my friends alone. They come over a lot to study or just watch TV. He bothers me and sometimes tells my friends things that are personal about me. Maybe he just wants attention, but it's very annoying. He should just grow up! Anyway, I told my mom and dad, but they say I need to solve the problem. **– Kathy**

4. I'm a neat person, and I used to live alone. I got a roommate a few months ago to help with the rent. The problem is, my roommate is not like me at all. He never does any chores around the house. He just sits around playing video games and watching TV. The apartment is always a mess, and I'm the one who has to clean it up. I can't count on him for anything. Should I just clean the apartment myself? This is a big problem for me. **– Daniel**

C Read the emails again. Who is each question about? Check (✓) the correct answers.

Who...?	T.J.	Marcy	Kathy	Daniel
lives with a messy person				
is a teenager				
is jealous of an animal				
is doing someone else's work				
lived alone last year				
mentions parents in the letter				

D PAIR WORK Have you ever had similar problems? What did you do about them? Tell your partner.

2 Listening On the air

A **Listen to the radio show *Addy's Advice*. What advice does Addy give to each person from Exercise 1? Check (✓) the correct answers.**

1 ☐ Show interest in the cat.
☐ Get a cat of your own.
2 ☐ Write your co-worker a note.
☐ Ask your co-worker to do things.
3 ☐ Go to someone else's house.
☐ Remind your parents of the situation.
4 ☐ Throw the roommate out.
☐ Communicate.

B **Listen again. Which statement does Addy probably agree or disagree with? Write A (agree) or D (disagree).**

1 People never lose interest in things over time. ______
2 Most people have problems with co-workers at some time. ______
3 Parents don't always need to solve their children's problems. ______
4 Look for a new roommate if you have a problem. ______

3 Writing A piece of advice

A **Choose an email from Exercise 1. Think of three pieces of advice.**

B **Write an email giving advice. Use the model and your ideas from Part A to help you.**

C GROUP WORK **Share your emails. Do you agree with the advice? What other advice can you give? Discuss your ideas.**

Dear T.J.,

I read your email, and I understand your problem. It is possible to be jealous of a cat! I think it's important to find things that you can do with your friend and Peaches. It's a good idea to…

4 Speaking Take it or leave it.

A **Imagine you have two relationship problems. Write two sentences about each one. Be creative!**

1. My friends never remember my birthday. I always remember theirs!
2. My parents don't trust me. I need to call them every three hours.

B GROUP WORK **Share your imaginary problems. Your group gives advice. Take turns.**

A: I have a problem. My friends never remember my birthday. I always remember theirs!

B: It's a good idea to help them remember. Why not send them reminders?

C GROUP WORK **Whose advice do you think you'd follow? Why? Tell your group.**

I can give advice about relationships.

Wrap-up

1 Quick pair review

Lesson A Brainstorm!
Make a list of tips for healthy family relationships. How many can you think of? You have five minutes.

Lesson B Test your partner!
Apologize to your partner for three different things. Can your partner accept your apologies in three different ways? Take turns. You have two minutes.

Lesson C Guess!
Speculate about a celebrity, but don't say his or her name! Can your partner guess who it is? Take turns. You have two minutes.

A: This person might win an award for his new movie.

B: Is it . . . ?

Lesson D Find out!
What is the best relationship advice your partner has ever received? Who gave the advice? You have two minutes.

2 In the real world

What advice do the experts give? Go online and find advice in English about one of these topics. Then write about it.

a jealous friend	a neighbor's noisy dog
a friend who talks too much	an annoying boss
a lazy husband or wife	an inconsiderate neighbor

Dealing with Jealous Friends

I found a website that gives advice about jealous friends. If you have a jealous friend, try to find out why the friend is jealous. Try to understand how your friend feels. It's a good idea to tell your friend about a time when you felt jealous, too. That way she will not feel alone or embarrassed. Tell your friend what you did to feel better. Another piece of advice on the website is . . .

10 Living your life

Lesson A
- Qualities for success
- Reflexive pronouns

Lesson B
- Advising against something
- Considering advice

Lesson C
- Separable phrasal verbs
- Second conditional

Lesson D
- Reading "A Walk Across Japan"
- Writing: An accomplishment

Warm Up

A Look at the pictures. What have the people accomplished?

B What are some of your accomplishments? What other things would you like to accomplish in your life?

A He taught himself.

1 Vocabulary Qualities for success

A 🎧 **Match the words and their meanings. Then listen and check your answers.**

1 bravery ____	a. the ability to develop original ideas
2 confidence ____	b. the belief that you can succeed
3 creativity ____	c. a commitment to something
4 dedication ____	d. the quality of showing no fear

5 enthusiasm ____	e. the ability to change easily
6 flexibility ____	f. a strong interest in something
7 talent ____	g. the ability to make good decisions
8 wisdom ____	h. the natural ability to do things well

B 🎧 **Complete the chart with the correct adjective forms for the nouns. Then listen and check your answers.**

Noun	Adjective	Noun	Adjective
bravery	*brave*	enthusiasm	
confidence		flexibility	
creativity		talent	
dedication		wisdom	

C PAIR WORK **Which qualities in Part A do you think people are born with? Which do they develop from experience or by watching others? Discuss your ideas.**

2 Language in context A success story

A 🎧 **Read the story of Yong-eun Yang. What did he do in 2009?**

4:21PM

WEB ENCYCLOPEDIA

Yong-eun Yang

In his late teens, South Korea's Yong-eun Yang, or "Y. E.," enjoyed lifting weights and hoped to own his own gym someday. But that dream died when he hurt himself in the gym. So at age 19, he took a part-time job at a golf course. He picked up golf balls and began to observe other players. He started to practice the game by himself late at night, and he even forced himself to get up early to be at the course by 5:00 a.m. for more practice. This is how Y. E. taught himself to play golf. His dedication and patience paid off. He became a professional golfer in 1995, and, in 2009, this talented man won his first championship, beating Tiger Woods.

B **What other qualities for success do you think Y.E. has?**

3 Grammar Reflexive pronouns

Use reflexive pronouns when the subject and object of a sentence refer to the same person or thing.
I hurt **myself** at work.
He taught **himself** to play golf.
They consider **themselves** brave.

By *with a reflexive pronoun means "alone."*
She traveled **by herself** to the United States.
Do you like to practice with another person or **by yourself**?

Personal pronouns	Reflexive pronouns
I	myself
you	yourself
he	himself
she	herself
it	itself
we	ourselves
you	yourselves
they	themselves

Complete the sentences with the correct reflexive pronouns. Then compare with a partner.

1 I drew a picture of ______________ in art class.
2 I like your new hairstyle. Did you cut it ______________?
3 I think you and Joe can fix the sink ______________. You don't need to hire a plumber.
4 They had a great time. They really enjoyed ______________.
5 My brother doesn't consider ______________ brave, but he is.
6 Heather wrote that by ______________. Nobody helped her.
7 We taught ______________ Spanish before we moved to Peru.
8 I hurt ______________ at the gym last week. My arm still hurts.
9 I took a trip by ______________. It helped me be more confident.

4 Pronunciation Stress shifts

Listen and repeat. Notice the stress shifts when some words change from nouns to adjectives.

creativity	dedication	enthusiasm	flexibility
creative	dedicated	enthusiastic	flexible

5 Speaking Self talk

A PAIR WORK **Interview your partner. Ask questions for more information. Take notes.**

- Have you ever hurt yourself?
- Do you consider yourself brave?
- Have you ever traveled by yourself?
- Have you ever taught yourself something?
- Are you enjoying yourself in this class?
- Do you consider yourself a flexible person?

B PAIR WORK **Tell another classmate about your partner.**

"William hurt himself once. He broke his foot."

6 Keep talking!

Go to page 144 for more practice.

I can talk about myself and my experiences.

B I'll give it some thought.

1 Interactions Giving and considering advice

A What do you do if you have too much work or studying to do? Do you talk to anyone?

B Listen to the conversation. What is Bryan thinking about doing? Then practice the conversation.

Marta What's wrong, Bryan?

Bryan Well, my job is just really stressful right now. My boss just seems to give me more and more work. It's not fair.

Marta That's not good.

Bryan Actually, I'm thinking about quitting and looking for another job.

Marta Really? I wouldn't recommend that.

Bryan Why not?

Marta Well, because you may not find something better. And that would just give you more stress. Have you thought about talking to your boss?

Bryan Not really.

Marta Why don't you try that? Maybe there is something he can do.

Bryan I'll see.

C Read the expressions below. Complete each box with a similar expression from the conversation. Then listen and check your answers.

Advising against something	Considering advice
______________________	______________________
I don't think you should do that.	I'll think about it.
I'm not sure that's the best idea.	I'll give it some thought.

D How would you respond? Write A (advise against it) or C (consider it). Then practice with a partner.

1 I think you should call the doctor. ______

2 I plan to study all night before my test. ______

3 I recommend that you stay home tomorrow if you don't feel well. ______

4 I think you should visit your grandmother this weekend. ______

5 I'm going to paint my house bright pink. ______

6 I'm not going to class tomorrow because I want to watch a soccer game. ______

2 Listening Maybe I'll do that.

A Listen to Tim give advice to three friends. What is each friend's problem? Check (✓) the correct answers.

Problems	Recommendations
1 ☐ She needs to get a full-time job. ☐ She wants to take more classes. ☐ She's thinking about quitting her job. ☐ She's not going to graduate.	
2 ☐ He doesn't have the money. ☐ He doesn't have a credit card. ☐ The leather jacket doesn't fit. ☐ His friend won't lend him any money.	
3 ☐ She takes too many breaks. ☐ She can't do a math problem. ☐ She drank too much coffee. ☐ Tim is driving her crazy.	

B Listen again. What does Tim tell each friend to do? Complete the chart with his recommendations.

3 Speaking Think about it!

A Imagine your friend wants to do the things below. What advice would you give? Write notes.

- Your friend wants to buy a new, expensive car. He doesn't have the money, and he doesn't know how to drive!
- Your friend wants to take two more classes. He's already taking five classes, and he has a part-time job!
- Your friend wants to go camping in the mountains by himself for a week. He's never gone camping before!

B PAIR WORK **Role-play the situations in Part A. Then change roles.**

Student A: Imagine you want to do the things in Part A. Tell Student B what you want to do and why. Consider his or her advice.

Student B: Advise Student A against doing the things in Part A and explain why. Recommend something else. Use your ideas from Part A.

A: *I saw this really awesome car yesterday! I think I'm going to buy it.*

B: *I'm not sure that's the best idea.*

A: *Why not?*

I can advise against something. ✓

I can consider advice. ✓

C What would you do?

1 Vocabulary Separable phrasal verbs

A Match the phrasal verbs and their meanings. Then listen and check your answers.

1	He won't talk about his job, so I don't **bring** it **up**. _____	a. donate
2	I got a bad grade on this essay. I need to **do** it **over**. _____	b. return money
3	I don't need these books. I might **give** them **away**. _____	c. mention
4	This is Lynn's camera. I need to **give** it **back**. _____	d. do again
5	Paul lent me some money. I need to **pay** him **back**. _____	e. return

6	Which one is Susan? Can you **point** her **out**? _____	f. do later
7	We can't have this meeting now. Let's **put** it **off**. _____	g. identify
8	This is serious. We need to **talk** it **over**. _____	h. not accept
9	I may buy that car, but I want to **try** it **out** first. _____	i. use
10	I have a job offer, but I plan to **turn** it **down**. _____	j. discuss

B PAIR WORK **What have you done over, talked over, paid back, tried out, or put off recently? Tell your partner.**

A: *Have you done anything over recently?*

B: *Yes, I have. I did my English homework over last night. I made a lot of mistakes the first time!*

2 Conversation I'm kind of broke.

A Listen to the conversation. What is Lucia thinking about doing?

Elliot I really like your camera.

Lucia Actually, it's my friend Ben's. I'm just trying it out this week. I need to give it back to him tomorrow.

Elliot It looks really expensive.

Lucia It is. I'm thinking about buying one, but I can't right now.

Elliot Why not?

Lucia Well, I'm kind of broke. If I had more money, I'd buy it.

Elliot It would be nice to be rich, wouldn't it?

Lucia Tell me about it. What would you do if you were rich?

Elliot Hmm . . . If I were rich, I'd travel. I'd give some money away, too.

Lucia That's nice.

B Listen to the rest of the conversation. Why does Lucia want a camera?

3 Grammar Second conditional

Second conditional sentences describe "unreal" or imaginary situations. Use a past tense verb in the if *clause (the condition). Use* would *in the main clause.*

What **would** you **do** if you **had** more money?

If I **had** more money, I **would buy** a camera.

Use were *for the past tense of* be *in the condition.*

Would you **travel** if you **were** rich?

Yes, I **would**. No, I **wouldn't**.

Yes. If I **were** rich, **I'd travel** a lot. No. I **wouldn't travel** a lot if I **were** rich.

A Complete the conversations with the correct words. Then compare with a partner.

1 A What __________ you __________ (do) if you suddenly __________ (become) rich?

B I __________ (quit) my job. Then I __________ (travel) for a few months.

2 A If a teacher __________ (give) you a good grade by mistake, what __________ you __________ (do)?

B I __________ (not / feel) right about it. I __________ (point) out the mistake.

3 A How __________ you __________ (feel) if a friend __________ (call) you late at night?

B I __________ (be) surprised, but I __________ (not / feel) angry.

4 A If you __________ (have) a relationship problem, who __________ you __________ (talk) to?

B I __________ (talk) about the problem with my best friend.

B PAIR WORK Ask and answer the questions in Part A. Answer with your own information.

4 Speaking What would you do?

A PAIR WORK Discuss the questions. Take notes.

- Where would you go if you had a lot of money?
- What would you give away if you were rich?
- What would you do if you saw your teacher or your boss at the supermarket?
- When would you turn down a job offer?
- Would you point out a mistake if a classmate made one? Why or why not?
- What would you do over if you had the chance?

B GROUP WORK Share your ideas with another pair. Are your ideas similar or different?

5 Keep talking!

Go to page 145 for more practice.

I can talk about imaginary situations.

D What an accomplishment!

1 Reading

A What do you think it would be like to walk across your country? Why?

B Read the interview. Why did Mary and Etsuko often have to walk between 30 and 40 kilometers a day?

4:21PM

A Walk Across Japan

Mary King and Etsuko Shimabukuro completed a 7,974-kilometer walk across Japan. Mary takes our questions about their incredible accomplishment.

Why did you walk across Japan?
The mapmaker Ino Tadataka *inspired* me. He spent 17 years *on and off* walking through Japan. He drew the country's first real maps.

How long did it take?
A year and a half. We walked from the island of Hokkaido, in the north, down to Okinawa. In Hokkaido, we walked about 40 kilometers a day, and on the other islands, about 30. We often had no choice about the distance because we had to find a place to sleep.

Describe a typical day.
There really wasn't one, but we tried to start by 7:00 a.m. and walk for 10 to 12 hours. Sometimes we had breakfast on the road. We had to be careful in Hokkaido because the bears there could smell our food. We saw bears twice, which was terrifying!

Did you walk every day?
No. We needed to do our laundry, check our email, and rest. Also, I wanted to interview people for my blog.

What were some of the best parts?
There were many! We stayed in a *haunted* guesthouse, walked on fire at a festival, and visited many wonderful hot springs.

Any low points?
You know, overall, we really enjoyed ourselves, but there were a lot of aches and pains along the way. The traffic could be scary because there weren't always sidewalks for *pedestrians*.

Did you ever think about *giving up*?
No, we never wanted to stop. Actually, I was sad when it ended. I wanted to walk from Okinawa back to Tokyo, but Etsuko said we had to accept that we accomplished our goal. It was time to go home.

Would you do it over again?
Definitely. I'd love to *retrace* our steps when I'm 80. But I've also set myself the goal of walking across the U.K. or India someday.

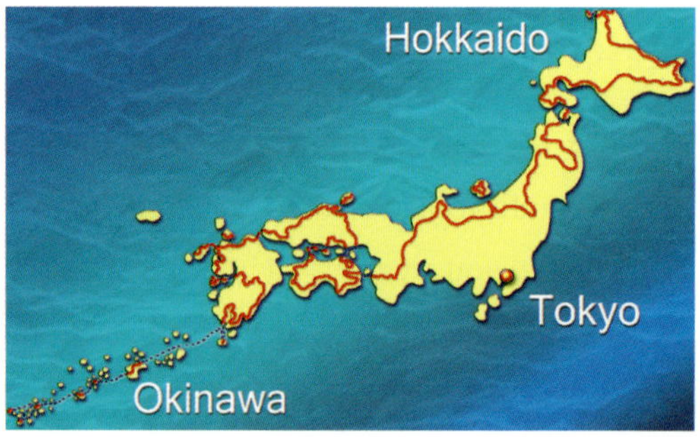

C Find the words in *italics* in the article. What do they mean? Write the words next to the correct definitions.

1. inhabited by ghosts ___haunted___
2. quitting ______
3. people who walk ______
4. go back over a route again ______
5. with breaks ______
6. gave someone an idea ______

D PAIR WORK How would you describe Mary's personality? Do you know anyone like her?

2 Listening Can I ask you . . .?

A Listen to four people talk about their biggest accomplishments this year. Write the accomplishments in the chart.

	Accomplishments	Qualities for success
1		
2		
3		
4		

B Listen again. What quality led to each person's success? Complete the chart.

C PAIR WORK Who do you think had the biggest accomplishment? Why? Discuss your ideas.

3 Writing An accomplishment

A Write a paragraph about something you accomplished in your lifetime. Use the questions and the model to help you.

- What did you accomplish?
- Why did you decide to do it?
- How did you accomplish it?
- What was challenging about it?
- Why was it important?

A Healthy Change

I decided that I wanted to change something at our school. A lot of the vending machines had very unhealthy food, like chocolate, candy, and potato chips. Students wanted healthier food like fruits and yogurt. So I asked students and teachers to sign a petition to get healthier food. It was difficult at first . . .

B GROUP WORK Share your paragraphs. How are your accomplishments similar or different?

4 Speaking What have you done?

CLASS ACTIVITY Find people who have done these things. Write their names and ask questions for more information.

Find someone who has . . .	Name	Extra information
helped someone with a challenging task		
won an award for doing something		
learned a new skill outside of school		
solved a problem at school, home, or work		
used technology to improve his or her English		

I can ask and talk about accomplishments.

Wrap-up

1 Quick pair review

Lesson A Test your partner!

Say three personal pronouns. Can your partner use the correct reflexive pronouns in sentences? Take turns. You have two minutes.

A: *He.*

B: *Himself. My neighbor introduced himself to me yesterday.*

Lesson B Do you remember?

Which sentences are advising against something? Check (✓) the correct answers. You have one minute.

- ☐ I don't think you should do that.
- ☐ Please don't worry about it.
- ☐ I'm not sure that's the best idea.
- ☐ I'll give it some thought.
- ☐ I'd rather not answer that.
- ☐ I wouldn't recommend that.

Lesson C Find out!

What is one thing both you and your partner would do in each situation? You have three minutes.

- Where would you go if you won a free vacation?
- What would you buy if you received money for your birthday?
- What would you do if you lost your cell phone?

Lesson D Brainstorm!

Make a list of accomplishments. How many can you think of? You have two minutes.

2 In the real world

Which country would you like to travel across? Go online and find information in English about one of these trips or your own idea. Then answer the questions and write about it.

a car trip across the United States	a train trip across Canada
a bike trip across France	a walking trip across England

- How far is it?
- How much would it cost?
- Where would you stay?
- How long would it take?
- What would you need to take?

A Road Trip in the U.S.A.

I'd take a car trip across the United States. I'd start in Ocean City, Maryland, and drive to San Francisco, California. The trip is about 3,000 miles. The first place I would stop is . . .

11 Music

Lesson A
- Compound adjectives
- Past passive

Lesson B
- Giving instructions

Lesson C
- Verb and noun formation
- Present perfect with *yet* and *already*

Lesson D
- Reading "A Guide to Breaking into the Music Business"
- Writing: A music review

Music Sales in the U.S.A.

"Source: www.statista.com, 2017"

Warm Up

A Label the pictures with the correct types of music from the chart.

B What do you think are the most popular kinds of music where you live? What's your favorite kind of music? What's your least favorite? Why?

A Music trivia

1 Vocabulary Compound adjectives

A Complete the compound adjectives with the correct participles. Then listen and check your answers.

Compound adjective	Present
award-__winning__ video	selling
best-______ artist	winning ✓
nice-______ voice	breaking
record-______ hit	sounding

Compound adjective	Past participle
high-______ ticket	downloaded
oddly ______ group	priced
often-______ performer	named
well-______ singer	known

B PAIR WORK Ask and answer questions with each phrase in Part A. Answer with your own ideas.

A: *Can you name an award-winning video?*

B: *Yes. Michael Jackson's video for "Thriller" won a lot of awards.*

2 Language in context Musical firsts

A Read about these musical firsts. Which musical firsts involved downloading?

Milestones in Music History

The first rap recording was made by the Sugarhill Gang. In 1979, the band's song "Rapper's Delight" became the first rap song to make the U.S. pop charts.

The song "Crazy" by Gnarls Barkley was leaked in 2005, months before its release. When it was finally released in March 2006, it became the first song to reach number one from downloaded sales.

The band Radiohead was the first to sell their album online for whatever people wanted to pay. Over a million albums were downloaded before the CD was released in December 2007.

The well-known band Aerosmith was the first to have a video game created around their music. People can play the guitar and sing along to 41 of their songs. The game was released in June 2008.

B What else do you know about these musical firsts? Do you know of any others?

"The band Run-DMC also recorded the song 'Rapper's Delight.'"

3 Grammar Past passive

The passive voice places the focus of a sentence on the receiver of an action instead of the doer of the action.

Active voice (simple past)
Fans **downloaded** over a million albums.

Passive voice (past of be *+ past participle)*
Over a million albums **were downloaded**.

Use the passive voice when the doer of the action is not known or not important.
The game **was released** in 2008.

When the doer of the action is important to know, use the passive voice with by.
The first rap recording **was made** by the Sugarhill Gang.

A Complete the sentences with the past passive forms of the verbs. Then compare with a partner.

1 All of the high-priced tickets to the concert ______ (sell) online.
2 The best-selling artists of the year ______ (give) a special award.
3 The singer's record-breaking hit ______ (write) by her mother.
4 The performer's biggest hit song ______ (use) in a TV commercial.
5 The band's award-winning video ______ (see) by millions of people.
6 The songs on her album ______ (play) with traditional instruments.

B PAIR WORK Say the trivia about the music group the Beatles. Your partner changes the sentences to use the past passive. Take turns.

1 In 1960, John Lennon suggested the name "the Beatles."
2 Ringo Starr replaced the original drummer, Peter Best, in 1962.
3 Paul McCartney wrote "Hey Jude" for John Lennon's son Julian.
4 Many people called George Harrison "the quiet Beatle."
5 *Rolling Stone* magazine chose the Beatles as the best artists of all time.

A: In 1960, John Lennon suggested the name "the Beatles."
B: In 1960, the name "the Beatles" was suggested by John Lennon.

4 Speaking Name it!

A Write three sentences in the past passive about the same song, singer, musician, band, or album, but don't use the name!

B GROUP WORK Share your sentences. Your group guesses the name of the song, singer, musician, band, or album. Take turns.

1. This singer's first album was called The Fame.
2. She was born in New York City.
3. She was made famous by her music and fashion statements.

(answer: Lady Gaga)

5 Keep talking!

Go to page 146 for more practice.

I can talk about music.

B The first thing you do is . . .

1 Interactions Giving instructions

A **What kinds of things do you use a computer for? How did you learn to do those things?**

B **Listen to the conversation. What steps does Amy follow to make a video playlist? Then practice the conversation.**

Tyler What are you doing, Mom?

Amy I'm trying to make a video playlist, but I'm not having much luck.

Tyler Let's see. First you need to create an account by typing in your information.

Amy OK. Thanks. Now what?

Tyler Next, search for the video you want to be first on your playlist.

Amy: All right. . . . Ah, here we go. How do I add it to a playlist?

Tyler Under the video, click *Add to* . . . and then choose *Create new playlist*. That's where you'll name your playlist and choose your privacy setting.

Amy Oh, look at that. Is that it?

Tyler Well, no. Finally, click *CREATE*.

Beginning instructions	Continuing instructions	Ending instructions
________	________	________
To start, . . .	Then . . .	To finish, . . .
The first thing you do is . . .	After that, . . .	The last thing you do is . . .

C **Read the expressions below. Complete each box with a similar expression from the conversation. Then listen and check your answers.**

D PAIR WORK **Number the instructions from 1 to 5. Then have a conversation like the one in Part B.**

How to download a ring tone:

_____ Click the *set ringtone* button to make the song your ring tone.

_____ Browse or search for a song in the app.

_____ Enjoy your new ringtone whenever your friends call you.

_____ Download the song you want to be your ringtone.

_____ Download a free ringtone app on your smartphone.

2 Listening How does it work?

A Listen to people give instructions on how to use three different machines. Number the machines from 1 to 3. There is one extra machine.

B Listen again. Each person makes one mistake when giving instructions. Write the mistakes.

1 She said ______________ instead of ______________.
2 He said ______________ instead of ______________.
3 She said ______________ instead of ______________.

C PAIR WORK Choose one of the machines above, and give instructions on how to use it. Add any additional instructions.

"To use a record player, first plug it in. Then…"

3 Speaking Step-by-step

A PAIR WORK Choose a topic from the list below or your own idea. Make a list of instructions about how to do it.

attach a file to an email
stream movies on a smartphone
create a playlist
download a podcast
make an international call
send a text message
upload a video

How to ______________
1.
2.
3.
4.
5.

B PAIR WORK Give your instructions to another classmate. Answer any questions.

A: *To attach a file to an email, first open your email account. After that, click "compose." Next, . . .*

I can give instructions.

C Music and me

1 Vocabulary Verb and noun formation

A Match the phrases and the pictures. Then listen and check your answers.

a	**announce** a tour	c	**compose** music	e	**perform** a song	g	**record** a song
b	**appreciate** music	d	**entertain** an audience	f	**produce** a song	h	**release** a new album

1 ☐ 

2 ☐ 

3 ☐ 

4 ☐ 

5 ☐ 

6 ☐ 

7 ☐ 

8 ☐ 

B Write the noun forms of the verbs in Part A. Then listen and check your answers.

a announcement c ________ e ________ g ________
b ________ d ________ f ________ h ________

C PAIR WORK Do you know any friends, artists, or other people who do or have done the things in Part A? Tell your partner.

2 Conversation I'm his biggest fan!

A Listen to the conversation. What does Andy tell Miranda to listen to?

Andy Oh, look! Richie Starr is going to perform here.
Miranda Yeah, I know. I'm planning to go.
Andy Really? Have you gotten a ticket yet?
Miranda Not yet. But I think you can still get them. I didn't know you were a fan.
Andy Are you kidding? I'm his biggest fan!
Miranda Have you heard his new album?
Andy He hasn't released it yet. But I've already downloaded his new single. Here, listen.
Miranda Nice! I hear he has a cool online fan club.
Andy He does. It gives information about new album releases and announces all upcoming performances.

B Listen to the rest of the conversation. Why didn't Andy know about the concert?

3 Grammar Present perfect with *yet* and *already*

In questions, use yet *when you expect the action to have happened.*	*In responses,* already *means the action has happened earlier.*	*In responses,* yet *means the action hasn't happened, but you expect it to.*
Have you **gotten** a ticket **yet**?	Yes, I**'ve already gotten** a ticket.	No, I **haven't gotten** a ticket **yet**.
Has he **released** his album **yet**?	Yes, he**'s already released** it.	No, **not yet**. He **hasn't released** it **yet**.

A **Write sentences in the present perfect with *already* and *yet* about a musician's goals. Then compare with a partner.**

1 He has already written four new songs.
2 ______
3 ______
4 ______
5 ______
6 ______

My Music Goals

- ☑ write four new songs
- ☐ record two songs for his album
- ☐ release his new album
- ☑ entertain children at the hospital
- ☑ give a free performance in the park
- ☐ announce his retirement

B PAIR WORK **Look at the musician's answers in Part A. Ask questions with *yet* and answer them.**

4 Pronunciation Syllable stress

A **Listen and repeat. Notice how the stress stays on the same syllable when these verbs become nouns.**

an**nounce**	enter**tain**	per**form**	pro**duce**
an**nounce**ment	enter**tain**ment	per**for**mance	pro**duc**tion

B **Listen. Circle the verb-noun pairs if the stress stays the same.**

appreciate	compose	record	release
appreciation	composition	recording	release

5 Speaking The latest

A CLASS ACTIVITY **Complete the questions with your own ideas. Then find someone who has already done each thing, and ask questions for more information.**

- Have you heard ______ (a new album or song) yet?
- Have you played ______ (a new video game) yet?
- Have you seen ______ (a new TV show or movie) yet?
- ______?

B GROUP WORK **Share your information.**

6 Keep talking!

Student A go to page 147 and Student B go to page 148 for more practice.

I can talk about things I've done recently.

D Making your own music

1 Reading

A What are music streaming sites? What sites do you listen to?

B Read the guide. Why do musicians have to market their music?

A Guide To Breaking Into The Music Business

In the past, successful music acts were supported by record labels that marketed and promoted their music. Although very few artists got high-priced recording contracts, it gave the artists a better chance to become well-known if they got "signed." Today, however, musicians all over the world are creating and recording their own music, and marketing it to fans without the help of record companies. Artists like Chance the Rapper, Glass Animals, and Anne-Marie have succeeded by making their music available to fans through streaming websites.

Here's how to take your self-made music directly to fans.

1. **Record.** If you haven't recorded something yet, you'll need to produce at least one great-sounding song and a music video to go with it.
2. **Upload.** Create a website where fans can download your music and find out how to follow you. You should also upload your music to streaming sites like Bandcamp, where music lovers go to discover new artists and bands.
3. **Market.** Go social. Try to gain followers on popular social media sites like Facebook, Twitter, Instagram, and Snapchat, and promote your music there. Don't forget to include links to your website.
4. **Track.** When someone wants to view, buy or download your song, be sure to have them like your site, follow you on Twitter or get their email address first. Then you can send them news and information about new releases and performances.
5. **Connect.** Use email, blogs, and social media to communicate with fans, giving them a personal connection to you, the artist.

Of course, now that anyone can take their music directly to fans, there is a lot more competition. Only a very few artists become rich and famous this way, but direct-to-fan marketing can help you find an audience that will appreciate your music.

C Read the guide again. Answer the questions.

1. In the past, how did artists become successful and well-known?
2. Where can artists promote their music now?
3. Why should musicians get email addresses of fans?
4. What does a musician need to do before marketing a song?
5. How do artists communicate with fans?

D PAIR WORK **What kind of music do you like? How do you discover new music, artists and bands?**

2 Writing A music review

A Write a review of an album (or a song) you'd recommend. Use the questions and the model to help you.

- What's the name of the album / song?
- When was it released?
- What do you like about the album / song?
- Is there anything you don't like about it?
- Why would you recommend it?

B CLASS ACTIVITY Post your reviews around the room. Read your classmates' reviews. Which songs or albums have you heard?

Momento

Bebel Gilberto's album *Momento* was released in 2007. All of the songs are good, but the title song is excellent. On the album, she blends Brazilian bossa nova with electronica and has a beautiful-sounding voice. The only thing I don't like about it is that there aren't enough songs! I'd recommend it because it was recorded with Japanese guitarist Masa Shimizu and . . .

3 Listening Song dedications

A Listen to five people call a radio show to dedicate songs to family members. Who do they dedicate songs to? Write the people in the chart.

	People	Song titles
1	friend	
2		
3		
4		
5		

B Listen again. What are the song titles? Complete the chart.

C PAIR WORK Imagine you can dedicate a song to someone. What song would you dedicate and to whom? Why? Tell your partner.

4 Speaking Soundtrack of my life

A Make a list of three songs that remind you of particular times or events in your life.

	Song titles	Memories
1		
2		
3		

B GROUP WORK Discuss your songs and memories. Ask and answer questions for more information.

A: The song . . . reminds me of middle school. It was my favorite song when I was 14.

B: I know that song! How do you feel now when you hear it?

A: Oh, I feel totally embarrassed. I can't stand it now!

I can talk about memorable songs.

Wrap-up

1 Quick pair review

Lesson A Brainstorm!

Make a list of words and phrases related to music. How many do you know? You have two minutes.

Lesson B Do you remember?

Complete the sentences with words or phrases to give instructions. You have one minute.

How to install software:

_________ find the software on its official website.

_________ download and click "install."

_________ restart your computer.

How to get money out of an ATM:

_________ put your ATM card in the machine.

_________ type in your code.

_________ select how much money you want.

Lesson C Find out!

What are two things both you and your partner have already done today? What are two things you both haven't done yet? You have three minutes.

Lesson D Test your partner!

Say (or sing) the words to a song you know in English. Can your partner guess the title and singer? You have two minutes.

2 In the real world

Who is your favorite singer? Go to the singer's website, and find information about his or her albums. Then write about them.

- What was the singer's first album? When was it released?
- When was the singer's last album released? Did it have any hit songs?
- What's your favorite song by this singer? What's it about?

Taylor Swift

My favorite singer is Taylor Swift. Her first album was called *Taylor Swift*. It was released in 2006. I love it. My favorite song on the album is called "Tim McGraw," who is a famous country music singer himself. Taylor was only sixteen years old when the song was released. The song is about how one of Tim McGraw's songs always reminds her of . . .

12 On vacation

Lesson A	Lesson B	Lesson C	Lesson D
• Vacation activities • Gerunds	• Asking about preferences • Reminding someone of something	• Extreme sports • Modals for necessity and recommendations	• Reading "A Taste of Cairo" • Writing: A walking tour

Kenji M

Kenji M added 4 new photos. 33 minutes ago
Best trip ever! Check out these amazing animals and beautiful beaches.

15 3

Kenji M added 2 new photos. December 17 at 9:47pm
The Grand Palace of Bangkok - wow!

18 1

Kenji M added 2 new photos. December 16 at 11:02pm
My first day here was all about great bargains and delicious food.

16 4

Warm Up

A Look at Kenji's social media posts. Where did he go on his vacation? What do you think he did there?

B What do you like to do on vacation? What kinds of things do you usually bring back with you?

A Travel preferences

1 Vocabulary Vacation activities

A Match the phrases and the pictures. Then listen and check your answers.

a buy handicrafts	c listen to live music	e speak a foreign language	g visit landmarks
b go to clubs	d see wildlife	f try local food	h volunteer

1 

2 

3 

4 

5 

6 

7 

8 

B PAIR WORK Which things in Part A have you *never* done on vacation? Tell your partner.

2 Language in context Three types of tours

A Read the ads for three tours. Which tour is best for someone who likes volunteering? Someone who likes eating? Someone who dislikes planning?

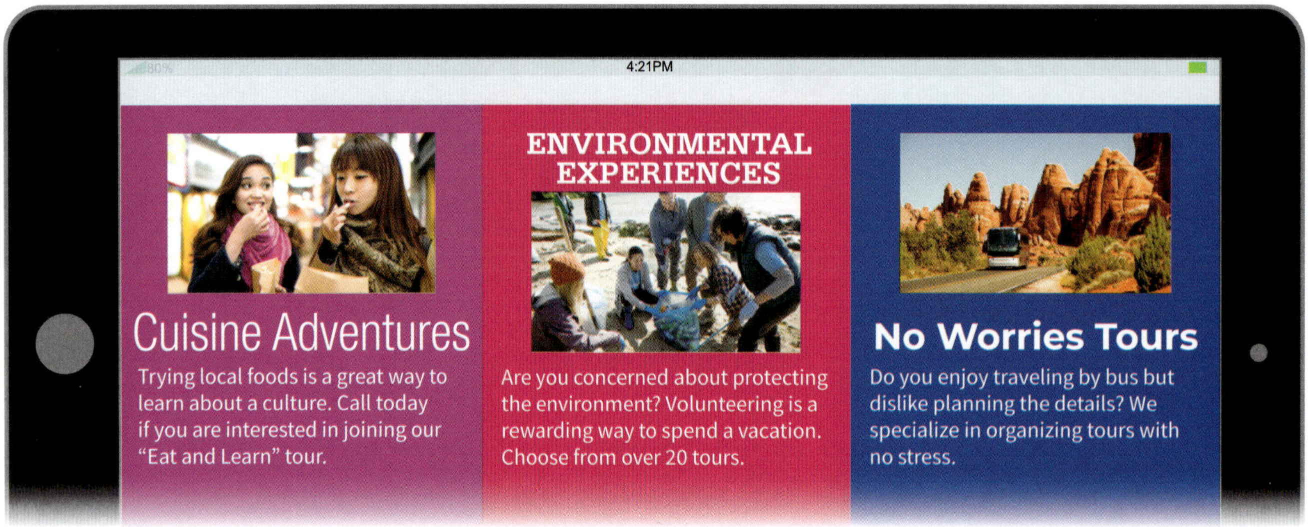

B What about you? Which tour interests you? Why?

3 Grammar Gerunds

A gerund is an –ing word that acts like a noun. Gerunds may be the subject of a sentence, or they may appear after some verbs or prepositions.

As subjects:	**Trying** local foods is a great way to learn about a culture. **Volunteering** is a rewarding way to spend a vacation.
After some verbs:	I **enjoy traveling** by bus. I **dislike planning** the travel details.
After prepositions:	I'm interested **in joining** the "Eat and Learn" tour. I'm concerned **about protecting** the environment.

A Complete the conversations with the gerund forms of the verbs. Then compare with a partner.

be buy get go help lose meet ✓travel try volunteer

1 A Do you enjoy ___traveling___ alone or in a group?
  B I prefer __________ in a large group. It's more fun.
2 A Are you interested in __________ handicrafts when you travel?
  B Not really. I like __________ to markets, but just to look.
3 A __________ local food is the best way to learn about a culture. Don't you agree?
  B I'm not really sure. __________ local people is also good.
4 A Are you worried about __________ sick when you travel abroad?
  B Not really. I'm more concerned about __________ my passport!
5 A Do you think __________ on vacation would be fun?
  B I do. __________ other people is a great thing to do.

B PAIR WORK Ask and answer the questions in Part A. Answer with your own information.

4 Speaking Travel talk

A Complete the questions with your own ideas. Use gerunds.

- Do you enjoy __________ when you're on vacation?
- Are you interested in __________ on vacation?
- Which is more interesting on vacation, __________ or __________?
- Are you ever concerned about __________ when you travel?
- As a tourist, is __________ important to you?
- __________?
- __________?

B GROUP WORK Discuss your questions. Ask and answer questions to get more information.

5 Keep talking!

Go to page 149 for more practice.

I can discuss travel preferences.

B Don't forget to . . .

1 Interactions Preferences and reminders

A Where do you usually stay when you travel? A hotel? A youth hostel?

B Listen to the conversation. What doesn't the guest need help with? Then practice the conversation.

Clerk Can I help you?
Guest Yes. I'm looking for a room for two nights.
Clerk Do you have a reservation?
Guest No, I don't.
Clerk Let me see what we have. Would you like a single room or a double room?
Guest A single is fine. I only need one bed.
Clerk I can give you room 13A. Please sign here. And there's a free breakfast from 7:00 to 9:00.
Guest Oh, great. Thank you very much.
Clerk Here's your key. Do you need help with your bag?
Guest No, that's all right.
Clerk OK. Remember to leave your key at the front desk when you go out.
Guest No problem.
Clerk Enjoy your stay.

C Read the expressions below. Complete each box with a similar expression from the conversation. Then listen and check your answers.

Asking about preferences

____

Would you prefer . . . or . . . ?

Would you rather have . . . or . . . ?

Reminding someone of something

____

Don't forget to . . .

Let me remind you to . . .

D Match the sentences and the responses. Then practice with a partner.

1 May I help you? ______
2 Would you like a single room? ______
3 Would you prefer a garden or an ocean view? ______
4 Please remember to lock your door at night. ______
5 Don't forget to check out by 11:00. ______

a. I don't know. Which one is cheaper?
b. Eleven? I thought it was by noon.
c. Actually, we need a double.
d. Yes. I have a reservation for one night.
e. I will. Thanks for the reminder.

2 Listening At a hostel

A Listen to a backpacker check into a hostel. Complete the form with the correct information.

Sydney Backpackers

Type of room:

☐ single ☐ double ☐ triple ☐ dorm

Number of nights? ________

Bathroom? ☐ yes ☐ no **Breakfast?** ☐ yes ☐ no

Method of payment:

☐ cash ☐ credit card

Room number: ________

B Listen again. Answer the questions.

1 Why doesn't she get a single room? ________
2 What time is breakfast? ________
3 What floor is her room on? ________
4 What does the receptionist remind her to do? ________

3 Speaking Role play

PAIR WORK **Role-play the situation. Then change roles.**

Student A: You want a room at a hotel. Student B is the clerk at the front desk. Circle your preferences. Then check in.

- You want a **single** / **double** room.
- You want to stay for **two** / **three** / **four** nights.
- You **want** / **don't want** your own bathroom.
- You **want** / **don't want** breakfast.

Student B: You are the clerk at the front desk of a hotel. Check Student A in. At the end, remind him or her of something.

B: Can I help you?
A: Yes, thank you. I'd like a room, please.
B: All right. Would you prefer a single or a double?
A: I'd prefer . . .
B: How many nights would you like to stay?
A: . . .
B: . . . And please don't forget . . .

I can ask about preferences.
I can remind someone of something.

C Rules and recommendations

1 Vocabulary Extreme sports

A 🎧 **Label the pictures with the correct words. Then listen and check your answers.**

bungee jumping	paragliding	skydiving	waterskiing
kite surfing	rock climbing	snowboarding	white-water rafting

1 ______ 2 ______ 3 ______ 4 ______

5 ______ 6 ______ 7 ______ 8 ______

B **PAIR WORK** **Which sports would you consider trying? Which wouldn't you do? Why not? Tell your partner.**

2 Conversation First-time snowboarder

A 🎧 **Listen to the conversation. Why does Sarah tell Kyle to stay in the beginners' section?**

Kyle Hi. I'd like to rent a snowboard, please.
Sarah OK. Have you ever been snowboarding?
Kyle Um, no. But I've skied before.
Sarah Well, we offer lessons. You don't have to take them, but it's a good idea. You'll learn the basics.
Kyle All right. When is your next lesson?
Sarah At 11:00. You've got to complete this form here to sign up.
Kyle No problem. What else do I need to know?
Sarah After your lesson, you should stay in the beginners' section for a while. It's safer for the other snowboarders.
Kyle OK. Anything else?
Sarah Yes. You must wear a helmet. Oh, and you ought to wear sunscreen. The sun can be very strong.

B 🎧 **Listen to the conversation between Kyle and his instructor. Why is Kyle uncomfortable?**

3 Grammar Modals for necessity and recommendations

Necessity	Recommendations
You **must** wear a helmet.	You**'d better** be back before dark.
You**'ve got to** complete this form.	You **ought to** wear sunscreen.
You **have to** listen to your instructor.	You **should** stay in the beginners' section.
Lack of necessity	You **shouldn't** go in the advanced section.
You **don't have to** take a lesson.	

A **Circle the best travel advice. Then compare with a partner.**

1. You **should** / **must** get a passport before you go abroad. Everybody needs one.
2. You **don't have to** / **'ve got to** visit every landmark. Choose just a few instead.
3. You **should** / **don't have to** book a hotel online. It's often cheaper that way.
4. You **ought to** / **shouldn't** get to your hotel too early. You can't check in until 2:00.
5. You **shouldn't** / **'d better** keep your money in a safe place. Losing it would be awful.
6. You **have to** / **should** pay for some things in cash. Many places don't take credit cards.
7. You **must** / **don't have to** show your student ID to get a discount. Don't forget it!
8. You **ought to** / **shouldn't** try some local food. It can be full of nice surprises!

B PAIR WORK **What advice would you give? Complete the sentences with modals for necessity or recommendations. Then compare answers.**

1. You ________________ go paragliding on a very windy day.
2. You ________________ have experience to go waterskiing.
3. You ________________ have special equipment to go bungee jumping.
4. You ________________ be in good shape to go kite surfing.

4 Pronunciation Reduction of verbs

A **Listen and repeat. Notice the reduction of the modal verbs.**

You've **got to** pay in cash. You **have to** check out by noon. You **ought to** try the food.

B PAIR WORK **Practice the sentences in Exercise 3. Reduce the modal verbs.**

5 Speaking Rules of the game

A GROUP WORK **Choose an extreme sport from Exercise 1. What rules do you think there are? What recommendations would you give to someone who wanted to try it?**

A: *You must sign a form before you go bungee jumping.*

B: *Yeah. And you should wear a helmet.*

C: *Oh, and you shouldn't be afraid.*

B CLASS ACTIVITY **Share your ideas.**

6 Keep talking!

Go to page 150 for more practice.

I can talk about rules and recommendations.

D Seeing the sights

1 Reading

A Do you ever read food or travel blogs? Do you ever watch food or travel TV shows?

B Read the blog. Write the headings above the correct paragraphs.

A Delicious Dinner	Juice Break	The Market	Sweet Shop

Home | About Arlen | My Blog | Q&A | Messages | Video | Recipes

A TASTE OF CAIRO

Cookbook author Arlen Gargagliano is always looking for new travel experiences. Join her on her blog as she takes a food tour of Cairo, Egypt.

__________ 1:45 p.m.

Today I walked through the narrow streets of a famous Cairo market. There were many areas to explore, but my favorite was the spice market. Each shop had huge containers of colorful spices. I bought a bag of mixed spices for a friend and some dark henna to dye my hair red!

__________ 3:15 p.m.

I stopped for one of my favorite drinks – sugar cane juice! A man took pieces of sugar cane, put them in a machine, and made juice. He gave me a glass of the juice, and I drank it quickly. It was sweet and delicious! It gave me lots of energy.

__________ 6:30 p.m.

I ate dinner at the Abou el Sid restaurant. I tried several appetizers. My two favorites were a creamy bean dish in a spicy sauce and fried eggplant with garlic. I had them with fresh flatbread. I also tried a famous Egyptian dish made with a green vegetable. I want to live in this place!

__________ 8:00 p.m.

Before walking back to the hotel, I made one last stop at a place that sells wonderful Egyptian sweets in el Hussein Square. It was busy, but I sat down and ordered a cup of tea and *basbousa*, a kind of cake made with semolina and sugar syrup. It was out of this world!

C Read the blog again. Write the initials of the blog headings (D, J, M, or S) in which Arlen did the activities below. (More than one answer is possible.)

1 ate a meal ______
2 bought a gift ______
3 drank something ______
4 had something sweet ______
5 saw spices ______
6 tried vegetables ______

D PAIR WORK Would you enjoy a tour like this? Why or why not? Discuss your ideas.

2 Writing A walking tour

A PAIR WORK **Choose a topic for an interesting walking tour in your town or city. Use one of the topics below or your own idea.**

architecture and design	historical sights	parks and nature
food and drink	nightlife	shopping

B PAIR WORK **Write a description of your walking tour.**

Historic Old San Juan

To really learn about the history of Puerto Rico, you have to walk through Old San Juan. You should start your walking tour at the city walls. Follow these walls along the sea to San Juan Gate, which was built around 1635. Go through the gate, turn right, and walk uphill. At the end of the street you can see La Fortaleza . . .

La Fortaleza
Old San Juan, Puerto Rico

C GROUP WORK **Present your tour to another pair. Did you include any of the same places?**

3 Listening An adventure tour

A **Listen to a guide talk to some tourists before a Grand Canyon rafting trip. What does the guide tell the tourists to do? Check (✓) the correct answers.**

☐ wear a safety vest	☐ wear sunscreen	☐ bring your cell phone
☐ drink a lot of water	☐ wear a hat	☐ wear a swimsuit
☐ bring water	☐ leave your camera	☐ wear tennis shoes
☐ bring food	☐ bring plastic bags	☐ listen to your guide

B **Listen again. Are the statements true or false? Write T (true) or F (false).**

1. The most important thing to remember is to have fun. ______
2. The tourists need to wear safety vests at all times on the raft. ______
3. There is no eating or drinking allowed. ______
4. The tourists shouldn't leave their phones on the bus. ______

4 Speaking Dream trip

A **Imagine you can go anywhere in the world for three weeks. Answer the questions.**

- What kind of trip are you interested in taking?
- What places would you like to visit? Why?
- What would you like to do in each place?
- How long do you plan to spend in each place?
- How can you get from place to place?

B PAIR WORK **Tell your partner about your dream trip. Ask and answer questions for more information.**

I can describe my dream trip. ✓

Wrap-up

1 Quick pair review

Lesson A **Test your partner!**

Say four vacation activities. Can your partner use the gerund form of the phrase in a sentence correctly? You have three minutes.

A: *See wildlife.*

B: *I'm not interested in seeing wildlife on vacation.*

Lesson B **Give your opinion!**

Ask your partner which vacation he or she prefers from each pair of pictures. Then remind your partner to do or take something on the trip. Take turns. You have two minutes.

A: *Would you prefer going to an island or to the mountains?*

B: *I'd prefer going to an island.*

A: *OK. Remember to take sunscreen.*

Lesson C **Brainstorm!**

Make a list of extreme sports people do in the water, in the air, and on land. How many do you know? You have one minute.

Lesson D **Guess!**

Describe your dream trip to your partner, but don't say where it is. Can your partner guess where it is? Take turns. You have two minutes.

2 In the real world

Go online and find recommendations in English for people who want to try a new sport. Use one of the sports below or your own idea. Then write about it.

sandboarding	downhill mountain biking	base jumping	bodyboarding

Sandboarding

Sandboarding is like snowboarding, but you do it on sand, not snow. You must have a sandboard for this sport. You should wear glasses so that you don't get sand in your eyes.

Finding out more

A **Read the chart. Then add two more.**

Find someone who . . .	Name	Extra information
is saving money for something special		
is in a good mood today		
has one brother and one sister		
is reading an interesting book		
wants to get a pet		
is taking a different class		
works on weekends		
thinks English is fun		
hates to talk on the phone		

B CLASS ACTIVITY **Find classmates who do or are doing each thing in Part A. Write their names. Ask questions for more information.**

A: *Are you saving money for something special?*

B: *Yes, I am.*

A: *Oh, really? What do you want to buy?*

C CLASS ACTIVITY **Share the most interesting information.**

Similar behaviors

A **Write your answers to the questions in the chart.**

Questions	Me	Name: ______
1 What do you do when you can't sleep at night?		
2 What do you do if you forget to do your homework?		
3 When you feel really happy about something, what do you do?		
4 What do you do if someone tells you something that isn't true?		
5 If a friend calls you and you don't want to talk, what do you do?		
6 What do you do when you are extremely angry at someone?		

B PAIR WORK **Interview your partner. Complete the chart with his or her answers.**

A: *What do you do when you can't sleep at night?*

B: *I usually read a book. How about you?*

A: *When I can't sleep at night, I always listen to music.*

C PAIR WORK **Compare your information. Do any of your partner's answers surprise you? Do you and your partner have any similar behaviors?**

What was happening?

A Look at this picture for two minutes. What was happening when it started to rain? Try to remember as many details as you can.

B PAIR WORK Cover the picture. Ask the questions and answer with the information you remember.

1 Where was the couple sitting when the rain started? What were they doing?
2 What was the police officer holding? What was she wearing?
3 What was the name of the café? What was on the café table?
4 What was the waiter holding? Where was he standing?
5 What was the young boy holding? What was he watching on TV?
6 What was the taxi driver doing? What was the name of the cab company?

C PAIR WORK Check your answers. How many answers did you remember correctly?

How does it end?

A PAIR WORK Imagine you are the people in one of the sets of pictures below. Tell a story that explains what happened. Choose your own ending to the story.

Story 1

Story 2

B GROUP WORK Tell your story to another pair. Can they think of another ending to your story? Which ending do you like better?

"This really happened to us. We were driving down the road in our car. The weather was very nice, and we were enjoying the ride. We were going to our friend's house. We had a map, but suddenly . . ."

C CLASS ACTIVITY Share your stories. Vote on the best one.

Then and now

Student A

A PAIR WORK You and your partner have pictures of Chuck. You have an old picture of what he used to look like, and your partner has a new picture of what he looks like now. Describe Chuck to find the differences between then and now.

Chuck – then

A: *Chuck used to have long black hair.*

B: *He doesn't have long hair now.*

A: *So that's different. He used to . . .*

B PAIR WORK You and your partner have pictures of Amy. You have a new picture of what she looks like now, and your partner has an old picture of what she used to look like. Describe Amy to find the differences between then and now.

Amy – now

Then and now

Student B

A PAIR WORK **You and your partner have a picture of Chuck. You have a new picture of what he looks like now, and your partner has an old picture of what he used to look like. Describe Chuck to find the differences between then and now.**

Chuck – now

A: *Chuck used to have long black hair.*

B: *He doesn't have long hair now.*

A: *So that's different. He used to . . .*

B PAIR WORK **You and your partner have pictures of Amy. You have an old picture of what she used to look like, and your partner has a new picture of what she looks like now. Describe Amy to find the differences between then and now.**

Amy – then

What's hot?

A PAIR WORK **Write your own example of each thing in the chart.**

Give an example of . . .	Me	Name:
something which looks tacky on young people		
an area of town that's extremely trendy		
a store that's very popular with young people		
a male celebrity who's really fashionable		
a female celebrity who's very glamorous		
a fashion trend that was very weird		
a fashion that you really like		
someone that has influenced fashion		

B PAIR WORK **Interview your partner. Complete the chart with his or her answers.**

A: What is something which you think looks tacky on young people?

B: Well, I don't like those big sunglasses that some young girls wear. I think they're tacky.

C CLASS ACTIVITY **Compare your information. Do you agree with everyone's opinion? Why or why not?**

A: I think . . . is a celebrity who's very glamorous.

B: Really? I think her clothes are kind of weird.

C: I like most of the clothes that she wears. I think she has a lot of style.

I've never . . .

A **Write examples of things you've never done.**

a sport I've never played:

___

a TV show I've never watched:

___

a food I've never eaten:

___

a famous movie I've never seen:

___

a restaurant I've never been to:

___

a place I've never visited:

___

B GROUP WORK **Tell your group about the things you've never done. Ask and answer questions for more information.**

A: *I've never played cricket.*

B: *Yeah, that's not popular here at all.*

C: *I've never played basketball.*

D: *You're kidding! Never? Not even in school?*

C CLASS ACTIVITY **Share your information. Which answers surprised you the most?**

No kidding!

A **Add two more questions about experiences to the chart.**

Have you ever . . . ?	Me	Name: ______
seen a solar eclipse		
watched three movies in one day		
gone swimming in the rain		
gotten a postcard from overseas		
cooked a vegetarian dinner		
seen a shooting star		
had a really bad haircut		
forgotten to pay an important bill		
eaten in a French restaurant		
lost something very special to you		

a solar eclipse

a shooting star

B PAIR WORK **Interview your partner. Complete the chart with his or her answers.**

A: *Have you ever seen an eclipse?*

B: *Yes, I have. I saw a solar eclipse once.*

A: *No kidding! When did you see it?*

C **Share the most interesting information.**

Impressive places

Student A

A You and your partner have information about impressive places. Do you know the answers to the questions on the left? Circle your guesses.

1 Which is taller?
   a. Eiffel Tower (Paris, France)
   b. CN Tower (Toronto, Canada)

a. ☐ 300.5 meters tall
b. ☐ ______________ meters tall

2 Which is longer?
   a. Golden Gate Bridge (San Francisco, the U.S.A.)
   b. Harbor Bridge (Sydney, Australia)

a. ☐ ______________ meters long
b. ☐ 1,149 meters long

3 Which is bigger?
   a. Red Square (Moscow, Russia)
   b. Tiananmen Square (Beijing, China)

a. ☐ 23,100 square meters
b. ☐ ______________ square meters

4 Which has more riders?
   a. São Paulo subway system (Brazil)
   b. London subway system (the U.K.)

a. ☐ ______________ riders a day
b. ☐ 4,250,000 riders a day

B PAIR WORK Ask and answer questions to fill in the missing information. Then check (✓) the correct answers in Part A.

How tall is . . . ?
How long is . . . ?
How big is . . . ?
How many riders does . . . have?

Saying large numbers

100.2	"one hundred point two"
3,456	"three thousand four hundred (and) fifty-six"
78,900	"seventy-eight thousand nine hundred"
120,000	"one hundred (and) twenty thousand"
3,450,000	"three million four hundred (and) fifty thousand"

C CLASS ACTIVITY How many of your guesses were correct? Can you make more comparisons?

unit 5 **Lesson C**

Planning a visit

A PAIR WORK **Imagine that a friend from another country is planning to visit you and asks you the questions in the email below. Discuss your responses.**

Reply Forward

To: Beth <bettybeth@email.com>
From: Jane <jgal@email.com>
Date: March 17
Subject: **Re: Planning my trip . . .**

Hey!
Before I visit, I have some questions for you:

- What's the best way to travel around? Is it the fastest? Is it the cheapest?
- Which part of town has the best nightlife? When is the best time to go out?
- What's the most popular place for a tourist to visit? Have you been there?
- What's the most interesting traditional food to try? Where should I try it?
- What would make a nice day trip? Is it easy to get to?
- What's the best museum? What's it like? Should I go there?
- Which time of year has the nicest weather? Which has the worst?

I'm sorry that I'm asking so many questions. I'm just very excited, and I want to plan as much as I can!

Thanks in advance for the information. See you soon!

Take care,
Jane

A: *The best way to travel around is by subway.*
B: *I think it's better to go by bus. It's faster than the subway.*

B GROUP WORK **Share your ideas with another pair. Do you have similar answers?**

Impressive places

Student B

A You and your partner have information about impressive places. Do you know the answers to the questions on the left? Circle your guesses.

1 Which is taller?
  a. Eiffel Tower (Paris, France)
  b. CN Tower (Toronto, Canada)

a. ☐ ________ meters tall

b. ☐ 553.3 meters tall

2 Which is longer?
  a. Golden Gate Bridge (San Francisco, the U.S.A.)
  b. Harbor Bridge (Sydney, Australia)

a. ☐ 2,737 meters long

b. ☐ ________ meters long

3 Which is bigger?
  a. Red Square (Moscow, Russia)
  b. Tiananmen Square (Beijing, China)

a. ☐ ________ square meters

b. ☐ 440,000 square meters

4 Which has more riders?
  a. São Paulo subway system (Brazil)
  b. London subway system (the U.K.)

a. ☐ 3,500,000 riders a day

b. ☐ ________ riders a day

B PAIR WORK Ask and answer questions to fill in the missing information. Then check (✓) the correct answers in Part A.

How tall is . . . ?
How long is . . . ?
How big is . . . ?
How many riders does . . . have?

Saying large numbers

100.2	"one hundred point two"
3,456	"three thousand four hundred (and) fifty-six"
78,900	"seventy-eight thousand nine hundred"
120,000	"one hundred (and) twenty thousand"
3,450,000	"three million four hundred (and) fifty thousand"

C CLASS ACTIVITY How many of your guesses were correct? Can you make more comparisons?

The next two weeks

Student A

A Complete the calendar for next week and the week after it with the correct dates and any plans you have.

Next week:

Sunday	Monday	Tuesday	Wednesday	Thursday	Friday	Saturday

The week after next:

Sunday	Monday	Tuesday	Wednesday	Thursday	Friday	Saturday

B PAIR WORK Ask and answer questions about your plans. Find a time to do something together.

A: *What are you doing next Thursday afternoon?*

B: *Oh, I have my karate lesson then. What are you doing the day after that?*

A: *Nothing. Do you want to get together?*

C GROUP WORK Tell another pair about the plans you made in Part B. Invite them to join you. Are they free?

A: *Barry and I are getting together on Friday.*

B: *We're meeting at Mr. Freeze for some ice cream. Do you want to join us?*

C: *I'm sorry, but I can't. I have a job interview on Friday*

D: *I'm not free, either. I have to go grocery shopping.*

unit 6 Lesson C

A helping hand

A PAIR WORK **Imagine you're the people in the pictures. Role-play the situations.**

Student A: Ask Student B for a favor.

Student B: Agree to Student A's request. Offer to help, and continue the conversation.

A: *Could you do me a favor? Could you please take my picture?*

B: *No problem. I'll take it for you.*

B PAIR WORK **Change roles. Role-play the new situations.**

C PAIR WORK **Ask each other for two more favors.**

Left brain / right brain

A PAIR WORK Interview your partner. Check (✓) his or her answers.

4:21PM

Left Brain vs. Right Brain

Do you use your right or left brain more often? Try this fun quiz and find out.

1 How do you remember things?
- ☐ a. with words
- ☐ b. with pictures
- ☐ c. both

2 Which can you remember easily?
- ☐ a. names
- ☐ b. faces
- ☐ c. both

3 Which math subject do you like?
- ☐ a. algebra
- ☐ b. geometry
- ☐ c. both

4 How do you like to work in class?
- ☐ a. alone
- ☐ b. in groups
- ☐ c. both

5 How do you like to study alone?
- ☐ a. quietly
- ☐ b. with music playing
- ☐ c. both

6 Which activity do you enjoy?
- ☐ a. writing
- ☐ b. drawing
- ☐ c. both

7 What kinds of tests do you like?
- ☐ a. multiple choice
- ☐ b. essay
- ☐ c. both

8 How do you like things explained to you?
- ☐ a. with words
- ☐ b. with actions
- ☐ c. both

9 What do you use to make decisions?
- ☐ a. the facts
- ☐ b. my experience
- ☐ c. both

10 How do you like to solve problems?
- ☐ a. one at a time
- ☐ b. at the same time
- ☐ c. both

11 How do you manage your time?
- ☐ a. very carefully
- ☐ b. not very carefully
- ☐ c. both

12 Which animals do you like?
- ☐ a. dogs
- ☐ b. cats
- ☐ c. both

Source: library.thinkquest.org

B PAIR WORK Score your partner's answers. Is he or she left-brained or right-brained? (More *c* answers or the same number of *a* and *b* answers means your partner has traits for both.)

More *a* answers: Left-brained	More *b* answers: Right-brained
More verbal than visual	More visual than verbal
Likes to do things step by step	Likes to do things at the same time
Very organized	Not always organized
Follows rules without questioning	Often asks why
Strong sense of time	Little sense of time
Learns by seeing	Learns by doing
Uses few gestures when talking	Talks with hands
Listens to what is said	Listens to how something is said

C GROUP WORK Do your results in Part B describe you well? What do you think your results say about your personality?

People on my mind

A **Write the name of someone you know for each description. Then think about answers to the questions.**

Someone I miss very much:

____

- How long have you known this person?
- When did you last see him or her?
- When will you see each other again?

Someone who gave me a special gift:

____

- What was the gift?
- How long have you had it?
- What made the gift special?

Someone I'd like to know better:

____

- How long have you known this person?
- When was the last time you spoke?
- What's he or she like?

Someone I've admired since I was a child:

____

- When did you first meet this person?
- What do you admire about him or her?
- Do you share any of the same qualities?

B PAIR WORK **Interview your partner about each person. Ask questions for more information.**

A: *Who is someone you miss very much?*

B: *I miss my grandmother very much.*

A: *How long have you known her?*

B: *I've known her since I was born! But I haven't seen her since April.*

A green quiz

A PAIR WORK Interview your partner. Circle his or her answers.

4:21PM

HOW GREEN ARE YOU?

Try this quiz to find out.

1 You're leaving for the weekend, but you're not taking your computer. What do you do?

a. Put it to "sleep."
b. Shut it down.
c. Turn it off and unplug it.

2 You're planning to go to a movie with several friends. What do you do?

a. Go in separate cars.
b. Meet and go in one car.
c. Take public transportation.

3 You're walking and you see some empty bottles on the sidewalk. What do you do?

a. Leave the bottles there.
b. Put them in a garbage can.
c. Put them in a recycling bin.

4 Your school has water fountains for people to drink from. What do you do?

a. Buy bottled water instead.
b. Drink directly from the water fountains.
c. Fill up your own water bottle.

5 You're buying a magazine, and the cashier starts to put it in a bag. What do you do?

a. Take the bag and throw it away later.
b. Take the bag, but reuse it.
c. Just take the magazine.

6 You have some old, unused medicine that you don't need. What do you do?

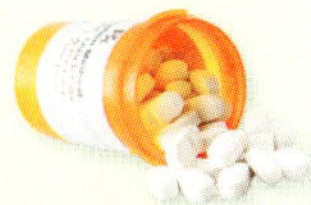

a. Flush it down the toilet.
b. Throw it in the garbage.
c. Return it to a pharmacy.

7 You're making a salad and realize you don't have enough lettuce. What do you do?

a. Get any lettuce at the nearest store.
b. Buy organic lettuce at a farmer's market.
c. Pick some lettuce from your own garden.

8 A company in your neighborhood is harming the environment. What do you do?

a. Nothing.
b. Tell your friends.
c. Write a letter to the local newspaper about it.

B PAIR WORK Score your partner's answers. How green is he or she? Are the results accurate?

a answers = 0 points	11–16 Congratulations! You lead a very green life.
b answers = 1 point	6–10 You're green in some ways, but not in others.
c answers = 2 points	0–5 You're not very green. It's not too late to change!

C PAIR WORK What other things do you do to help the environment? Tell your partner.

Be an optimist!

A PAIR WORK **Add two situations to the chart. Then discuss what will, could, or might happen in each situation. Take notes.**

If we . . . ,	we will . . .	we might . . .
eat too much fast food		
spend all day at the beach		
use cell phones in class		
read the news every day		
never study English		
watch too much TV		
don't get enough sleep		
spend too much time online		

A: *What do you think will happen if we eat too much fast food?*

B: *If we eat too much fast food, we'll gain weight.*

B GROUP WORK **Share your ideas with another pair. Which ideas are the best? Do you have any other ideas?**

What to do?

A GROUP WORK **Imagine you have one of the relationship problems below. Your group gives you advice. Take turns.**

My friend texts me constantly and then gets angry if I don't answer right away. Is it important to answer every text? I'm not sure what to do about this. I prefer to communicate by phone.

My sister has a new hairstyle, and I think it looks pretty awful. I don't really want to criticize her, but I think it's a good idea to say something to her. But what exactly do I say?

My co-worker won't talk to me. She says I gossiped about her. I guess I did, but it wasn't anything serious. It feels like she's judging me. I hope she can forgive me. After all, we need to work together.

My classmate always tries to copy my answers when we are taking tests or working on our own. It makes me angry. I don't want the teacher to think I'm cheating, too. Should I tell my teacher?

A: *My friend texts me constantly and then . . .*

B: *It's not important to answer every text. Just ignore them.*

C: *But it's not good to ignore them. Say something to your friend about it.*

D: *That's good advice. It's also a good idea to . . .*

B GROUP WORK **Which advice was the best? Why? Tell your group.**

"Maria gave the best advice. It's important to tell the truth."

C GROUP WORK **Have you ever given relationship advice to someone? Who? What was the advice? Tell your group.**

What do you think?

A PAIR WORK Look at the picture. Make one speculation about each person. Use *must*, *could*, *can't*, *may*, or *might*.

A: Diego is buying a dress, but it can't be for his wife. It's too small.

B: Right. He might be buying it for his daughter.

A: Yeah. And he must be rich. The store looks very expensive.

B GROUP WORK **Compare your speculations with another pair. Did you make any of the same ones?**

Reflections

A CLASS ACTIVITY **Find classmates who answer "yes" to each question. Write their names and ask questions for more information.**

Questions	Name	Extra information
1 Have you ever eaten an entire pizza by yourself?		
2 Do you learn better by studying in a group than by yourself?		
3 Did you teach yourself how to cook?		
4 Do you see yourself living in another country in five years?		
5 Have you ever traveled anywhere by yourself?		
6 Would you like to change something about yourself?		
7 Have you ever lived by yourself?		
8 Do you know someone who taught himself or herself a foreign language?		

A: *Have you ever eaten an entire pizza by yourself?*

B: *Yes, I have!*

A: *Wow! That's a lot of pizza. What kind of pizza was it?*

B: *It had cheese, pepperoni, onions, and peppers on it.*

B **Share your information. What's the most interesting thing you learned? Who else in the class answered "yes" to each question?**

Imagine that!

A Guess your partner's answers to the questions. Write your guesses in the chart.

Questions	My guesses	My partner's answers
1 What would you do if you saw your favorite celebrity?		
2 What would you do if your best friend moved to another country?		
3 How would you feel if someone brought up something embarrassing about you at a party?		
4 What would you do if you broke something expensive in a store?		
5 Where would you go if you had one week to travel anywhere in the world?		
6 What would you do if a friend borrowed some money from you and then didn't pay you back?		
7 What would you do if your grades in this class suddenly dropped?		

B PAIR WORK **Interview your partner. Complete the chart with his or her answers. How many of your partner's answers did you guess correctly?**

C CLASS ACTIVITY **Do any of your partner's answers surprise you? Would you and your partner do any similar things? Tell the class.**

Facts and opinions

A GROUP WORK **Add two sets of questions about music to the list. Then discuss the questions. Ask follow-up questions to get more information.**

1 What bands were formed in the 1960s? '70s? '80s? '90s? What was their music like?
2 What male singer do you think has a nice-sounding voice? What female singer?
3 What well-known singers or bands do you not like very much? Why not?
4 Were any record-breaking hits released last year? What did you think of the songs?
5 Was any truly awful music released in the past few years? What made it so terrible?
6 What was the last music awards show you saw on TV? Who was on it?
7 Who are the best-selling singers from your country? Do you enjoy their music?
8 What are some easily learned songs in your native language? Do you know all the words?
9 ______? ______?
10 ______? ______?

The Rolling Stones, 1960s

ABBA, 1970s

R.E.M., 1980s

The Spice Girls, 1990s

A: *The Rolling Stones were formed in the 1960s.*
B: *How was their music?*
A: *Their music was fantastic. It still is.*
C: *Can you name the band members?*

B CLASS ACTIVITY **Share any interesting information.**

Find the differences

Student A

You and your partner have pictures of Monica and Victor, but they aren't exactly the same. Ask questions with *yet* to find the differences. Circle the items that are different.

see a movie

get a new TV

download a song

send a text

buy a video game

sing a song

A: Have Monica and Victor seen a movie yet?

B: No, they haven't. In my picture, they haven't seen it yet. They're going inside.

A: So that's different. In my picture, they're leaving the movie theater.

unit 11 **Lesson C**

Find the differences

Student B

You and your partner have pictures of Monica and Victor, but they aren't exactly the same. Ask questions with *yet* to find the differences. Circle the items that are different.

see a movie

get a new TV

download a song

send a text

buy a video game

sing a song

A: Have Monica and Victor seen a movie yet?

B: No, they haven't. In my picture, they haven't seen it yet. They're going inside.

A: So that's different. In my picture, they're leaving the movie theater.

Travel partners

A Add three questions about travel preferences to the chart. Then check (✓) your answers.

	When you travel, . . .	Me		Name: ______	
		Yes	**No**	**Yes**	**No**
1	do you like being in a large group?	☐	☐	☐	☐
2	are you interested in meeting new people?	☐	☐	☐	☐
3	is saving money important to you?	☐	☐	☐	☐
4	do you like trying new foods?	☐	☐	☐	☐
5	is asking directions embarrassing to you?	☐	☐	☐	☐
6	do you like knowing your schedule in advance?	☐	☐	☐	☐
7	is camping more fun than staying in hotels?	☐	☐	☐	☐
8	do you enjoy shopping for souvenirs?	☐	☐	☐	☐
9	do you like big cities?	☐	☐	☐	☐
10	do you like going to clubs?	☐	☐	☐	☐
11	is seeing everything possible important to you?	☐	☐	☐	☐
12		☐	☐	☐	☐
13		☐	☐	☐	☐
14		☐	☐	☐	☐

B PAIR WORK **Interview your partner. Complete the chart with his or her answers.**

C PAIR WORK **Compare your answers. Would you make good travel partners? Why or why not?**

A: *We wouldn't make good travel partners. You like being in a large group. I don't.*

B: *Yes, but we're both interested in meeting new people.*

A: *Well, that's true. And saving money is important to us.*

A backpacking trip

A PAIR WORK Imagine someone is planning a two-week backpacking trip to your country. What rules and recommendations would you give for each category? Take notes.

Packing	Communication
Health and safety	**Places to stay**
Transportation	**Money**
Food	**Other**

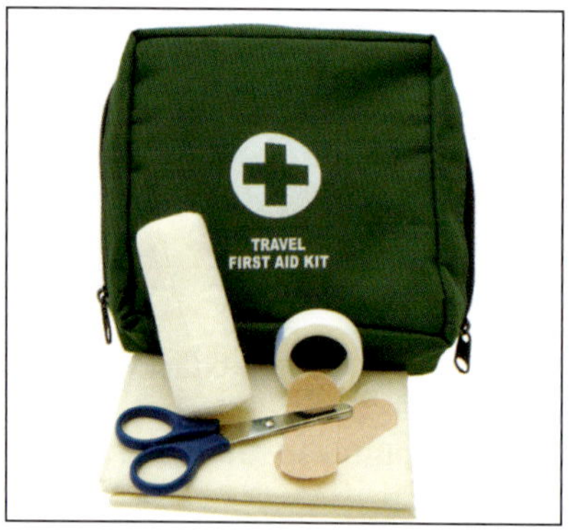

B GROUP WORK Share your ideas with another pair. Did you have any of the same rules or recommendations? Can you think of any other rules or recommendations?

A: *You shouldn't pack too many clothes.*

B: *Yes, but you have to have enough clothes!*

C: *Also, you ought to bring your cell phone.*

Irregular verbs

Base form	Simple past	Past participle
be	was, were	been
become	became	become
break	broke	broken
build	built	built
buy	bought	bought
choose	chose	chosen
come	came	come
do	did	done
draw	drew	drawn
drink	drank	drunk
drive	drove	driven
eat	ate	eaten
fall	fell	fallen
feel	felt	felt
fly	flew	flown
forget	forgot	forgotten
get	got	gotten
give	gave	given
go	went	gone
hang	hung	hung
have	had	had
hear	heard	heard
hold	held	held
know	knew	known
leave	left	left

Base form	Simple past	Past participle
lose	lost	lost
make	made	made
meet	met	met
pay	paid	paid
put	put	put
read	read	read
ride	rode	ridden
run	ran	run
say	said	said
see	saw	seen
sell	sold	sold
send	sent	sent
sing	sang	sung
sit	sat	sat
sleep	slept	slept
speak	spoke	spoken
spend	spent	spent
stand	stood	stood
swim	swam	swum
take	took	taken
teach	taught	taught
think	thought	thought
wear	wore	worn
win	won	won
write	wrote	written

Adjective and adverb formations

Adjectives	Adverbs
agreeable	agreeably
amazing	amazingly
ambitious	ambitiously
angry	angrily
brave	bravely
careful	carefully
confident	confidently
considerate	considerately
creative	creatively
curious	curiously
decisive	decisively
disagreeable	disagreeably
dishonest	dishonestly
early	early
easy	easily
enthusiastic	enthusiastically
extreme	extremely
fair	fairly
fashionable	fashionably
fast	fast
fortunate	fortunately
glamorous	glamorously
good	well
hard	hard
honest	honestly

Adjectives	Adverbs
immature	immaturely
impatient	impatiently
inconsiderate	inconsiderately
indecisive	indecisively
interesting	interestingly
late	late
lucky	luckily
mature	maturely
nervous	nervously
optimistic	optimistically
patient	patiently
quick	quickly
rare	rarely
reliable	reliably
sad	sadly
serious	seriously
similar	similarly
strange	strangely
stubborn	stubbornly
sudden	suddenly
surprising	surprisingly
unfair	unfairly
unfortunate	unfortunately
unreliable	unreliably
wise	wisely

Answer Key

Unit 7 Lesson D (page 71)

Listening

This personality test is just for fun. Don't take the answers *too* seriously!

1 This person is the most important person in your life.
2 If you see a big animal, you think you have big problems.
3 If you have a big house, you are very ambitious.
4 If the door is open, you're happy for people to visit anytime. If it's closed, you prefer people to call first.
5 If there is food or flowers on the table, you are very optimistic.
6 If the material is strong (like metal or plastic), you have a strong relationship with the person in number 1.
7 If you keep the cup, you want to keep a good relationship with the person in number 1.

Credits

The authors and publishers acknowledge the following sources of copyright material and are grateful for the permissions granted. While every effort has been made, it has not always been possible to identify the sources of all the material used, or to trace all copyright holders. If any omissions are brought to our notice, we will be happy to include the appropriate acknowledgements on reprinting and in the next update to the digital edition, as applicable.

Photography

All the photographs are sourced from Getty Images.

U1: Steve Debenport/E+; Hero Images; PeopleImages/DigitalVision; sturti/E+; Kwanchai Lerttanapunyaporn/EyeEm; ArisSu/iStock/Getty Images Plus; bonniej/E+; Tim Hall/Cultura; Lee Pettet/Stockbyte; Ca-ssis/iStock/Getty Images Plus; kali9/E+; studo58/iStock/Getty Images Plus; Peter Zvonar/Moment Open; paylessimages/iStock/Getty Images Plus; Caiaimage/Sam Edwards; James Griffiths Photography/iStock/Getty Images Plus; David Buffington/Photographer's Choice; 9wut/iStock/Getty Images Plus; trekandshoot/iStock/Getty Images Plus; Design Pics/Craig Tuttle; Chris Ryan/OJO Images; Rob Lewine; Maksim Kamyshanskii/iStock/Getty Images Plus; winhorse/iStock/Getty Images Plus; JGI/Jamie Grill/Blend Images; Lívia Fernandes - Brazil./Moment; Imgorthand/E+; BONNINSTUDIO/iStock/Getty Images Plus; ColorBlind Images/The Image Bank; quavondo/E+; **U2:** Blend Images - KidStock/Brand X Pictures; Geber86/E+; KatarzynaBialasiewicz/iStock/Getty Images Plus; PeopleImages/E+; Eric Audras/ONOKY; Tetra Images; groveb/iStock/Getty Images Plus; KiraVolkov/iStock/Getty Images Plus; Paul Bradbury/OJO Images; Erik Dreyer; Caiaimage/Tom Merton; Peter Dazeley/Photographer's Choice; Buena Vista Images/DigitalVision; PeopleImages/DigitalVision; George Doyle/Stockbyte; Lew Robertson/Corbis; ©David J Spurdens; Fuse; Juanmonino/E+; Jupiterimages/The Image Bank; Frank Fell/robertharding; cirano83/iStock/Getty Images Plus; Peter Dazeley/Photographer's Choice; MASSIVE/Stone; Image Source/DigitalVision; Peter Dazeley/Photographer's Choice; **U3:** Hoxton/Tom Merton; Eamonn McCormack/BFC/Getty Images Entertainment; Jake Curtis/Iconica; Lorado/E+; castillodominici/iStock/Getty Images Plus; Peter Dazeley/Photographer's Choice; Trinette Reed; Tvi Nguyen/EyeEm; Chauncey James/EyeEm; Dirk Saeger/EyeEm; CraigRJD/iStock/Getty Images Plus; Yagi Studio/DigitalVision; Nemia Walter/EyeEm; Phil Boorman/Cultura; Christophel Fine Art/UIG via Getty Images; The Art Collector/Print Collector; Brandon Colbert Photography/Moment; istanbulimage/E+; yasinguneysu/iStock/Getty Images Plus; ksevgi/iStock/Getty Images Plus; stuartbur/iStock/Getty Images Plus; nortongo/iStock/Getty Images Plus; NAKphotos/iStock/Getty Images Plus; Kay-Paris Fernandes/WireImage; Tetra Images; andresr/E+; Indeed; Mimi Haddon/DigitalVision; Morsa Images/DigitalVision; PeopleImages/E+; photosindia; fotostorm/E+; feedough/iStock/Getty Images Plus; Viktoria Ovcharenko/iStock/Getty Images Plus; FangXiaNuo/E+; Michele Quattrin; mQn Photography/Moment; soleg/iStock/Getty Images Plus; Vincent Besnault/Photographer's Choice; Fabrice LEROUGE/ONOKY; **U4:** RelaxFoto.de/E+; Graiki/Moment; Alexander Jackson/EyeEm; Ben Edwards/The Image Bank; gpointstudio/iStock/Getty Images Plus; guruXOOX/iStock/Getty Images Plus; TAGSTOCK1/iStock/Getty Images Plus; kali9/E+; Ivanko_Brnjakovic/iStock/Getty Images Plus; andresr/iStock/Getty Images Plus; Macduff Everton/The Image Bank; Cultura RM Exclusive/Frank and Helena; Martin Harvey/Photolibrary; Christian Kober/robertharding; Paul Poplis/Photolibrary; Ron Watts/All Canada Photos; Darryl Leniuk/The Image Bank; Carso80/iStock Editorial/Getty Images Plus; massimo colombo/Moment; Stewart Cohen/Blend Images; James Osmond/Photolibrary; kimkole/iStock/Getty Images Plus; PeopleImages/DigitalVision; LWA/Dann Tardif/Blend Images; StockFood; James Bruntz/Moment; Trinette Reed/Blend Images; Ricardo Liberato/Moment; DAVID NUNUK/Science Photo Library; Carlos Fernandez/Moment; **U5**: Photographer Henna Malik/Moment; Ibon Bastida/EyeEm; Dan77/iStock/Getty Images Plus; Guillaume CHANSON/Moment; Mark Miller Photos/DigitalVision; Lauren Bates/Moment Unreleased; Patricia Hamilton/Moment; Ilan Shacham/Moment; Tina Llorca/EyeEm; QQ7/iStock/Getty Images Plus; Pley/iStock/Getty Images Plus; David Madison/Corbis; Kadshah Nagibe/EyeEm; De Agostini Picture Library; Alexander Spatari/Moment; Christophe Launay/Aurora; JAWOC/AFP; Fuse; Marka/Universal Images Group; Santiago Urquijo/Moment; Ivan_off/iStock/Getty Images Plus; Alexander Bennett/EyeEm; Tunach/iStock/Getty Images Plus; grebcha/iStock/Getty Images Plus; Reinhard Dirscherl/WaterFrame; View Stock; IndiaPictures/Universal Images Group; JaySi/iStock/Getty Images Plus; Michele Falzone/The Image Bank; Jason Maehl/Aurora; Torresigner/iStock/Getty Images Plus; DeAgostini/G. SIOEN; Andrew Watson/The Image Bank; halecr/E+; Arctic-Images/Corbis Documentary; Tammy616/iStock/Getty Images Plus; Kodiak Greenwood/The Image Bank; Antonello/Moment Open; Matteo Colombo/DigitalVision; Roberto Machado Noa/LightRocket; Justin Sullivan/Getty Images News; xavierarnau/E+; DEA/W. BUSS/De Agostin; Lintao Zhang/Getty Images Entertainment; Victor Moriyama/Getty Images News; Photography taken by Mario Gutiérrez./Moment; Medioimages/Photodisc; **U6**: denozy/iStock/Getty Images Plus; White Packert/The Image Bank; Geber86/E+; Sam Edwards/OJO Images; skynesher/E+; Rob Daly/OJO Images; Terry Vine/Blend Images; Education Images/Universal Images Group; Blue Jean Images; PeopleImages/E+; LeoPatrizi/E+; Warren Photography/Warren Photography; JGI/Jamie Grill/Blend Images; kali9/iStock/Getty Images Plus; Westend61; Oleh_Slobodeniuk/E+; filadendron/E+; blackred/E+; Westend61; alikemalkarasu/E+; xxmmxx/E+; Wavebreakmedia/iStock/Getty Images Plus; Klaus Vedfelt/Riser; Erik Isakson/Blend Images; **U7**: sanjeri/E+; VCG/Contributor/Visual China Group; Kevin Dodge/Corbis; Jamie Grill; Lorado/E+; Lumina Images/Blend Images; powerofforever/E+; Tribalium/iStock; Hill Creek Pictures/UpperCut Images; Steve Debenport/E+; Cate Gillon/Staff/Getty Images News; Kathy Collins/Photographer's Choice; MatiasEnElMundo/iStock/Getty Images Plus; DreamPictures/The Image Bank; MangoStar_Studio/iStock/Getty Images Plus; Westend61; Jose Luis Pelaez Inc/Blend Images; **U8**: Erik Von Weber; Coldimages/iStock/Getty Images Plus; grafvision/iStock/Getty Images Plus; catalby/iStock/Getty Images Plus; Michel Tripepi/EyeEm; drnadig/E+; Krakozawr/E+; Elenathewise/iStock/Getty Images Plus; baona/iStock/Getty Images Plus; Michael Burrell